ce Bushnell - Robert De Niro - Franco - Jack
ind - Steve McCurry - Jay McInerney - t and
ne - Martin Scorsese - Taylor Swift - W dia
De Niro - James Franco - Jack Huston - Siri Hustvedt
cInerney - Moby - Robert and Cortney Novogratz - Yoko
- Taylor Swift -Woody Allen - Lidia Bastianich - Mario
co - Jack Huston - Siri Hustvedt - Spike Lee - Daniel
rt and Cortney Novogratz - Yoko Ono - Al Pacino - Cathleen
n - Lidia Bastianich - Mario Batali - Candace Bushnell -
tvedt - Spike Lee - Daniel Liebeskind - Steve McCurry
o Ono - Al Pacino - Cathleen Schine - Martin Scorsese
ali - Candace Bushnell - Robert De Niro - James
niel Liebeskind - Steve McCurry - Jay McInerney - Moby -
i Pacino - Cathleen Schine - Martin Scorsese - Taylor Swift
shnell - Robert De Niro - James Franco - Jack Huston - Siri
urry - Jay McInerney - Moby - Robert and Cortney Novogratz
sese - Taylor Swift - Woody Allen - Lidia Bastianich
- James Franco - Jack Huston - Siri Hustvedt - Spike Lee -
- Moby - Robert and Cortney Novogratz - Yoko Ono - Al
Woody Allen - Lidia Bastianich - Mario Batali -
Huston - Siri Hustvedt - Spike Lee - Daniel Liebeskind
d Cortney Novogratz - Yoko Ono - Al Pacino - Cathleen
Lidia Bastianich - Mario Batali - Candace Bushnell
stvedt - Spike Lee - Daniel Liebeskind - Steve McCurry
Yoko Ono - Al Pacino - Cathleen Schine - Martin Scorsese
rio Batali - Candace Bushnell - Robert De Niro - James
Liebeskind - Steve McCurry - Jay McInerney - Moby

And New York is the most beautiful city in the world?
It is not far from it. No urban night is like the night there.
I have looked down across the city from high windows.
It is then that the great buildings lose reality and take
on their magical powers [...]
Squares after squares of flame, set and cut into the aether.
Here is our poetry, for we have pulled down the stars to our will.

EZRA POUND

Project Editor
VALERIA MANFERTO DE FABIANIS

Editorial Coordination
LAURA ACCOMAZZO

Graphic Design
CLARA ZANOTTI

Graphic Layout
MARIA CUCCHI

MY
NEW YORK

Celebrities Talk about the City

Text by
ALESSANDRA MATTANZA

WHITE STAR PUBLISHERS

MY NEW YORK

Contents

ALESSANDRA MATTANZA
The "Author" of the City

"I love New York as I found it one of the most tolerant and welcoming cities in the world. I have lived in many cities in my life, and in some of them I always felt I was a foreigner. I was accepted, but I was always something 'strange and exotic' coming from another country with another background.

"In New York the people can sometimes be hard and tough, but they made me feel like a New Yorker after only one week of living here. And it is this incredible spirit of New York, which is like an incredible puzzle of faces and traditions from all over the world, of immigrants arriving here with a few dollars in their pocket but who believed in their dreams and their vision and in the American Dream, that makes this metropolitan city so special.

"In this book, you will find the vision and feelings of 'My New York', of people who have mostly been born and raised here, but also of the new New Yorkers, the ones who arrived here, who have been here a while, be it long or short, who live between here and LA who were struck by the magic spell of the thousand lights or of the reality of the street life, of its sidewalks and neighborhoods. Whose lives were changed or were amazed by New York, which will be always vibrant in them like the blood pulsing in their veins."

ALESSANDRA MATTANZA

Introduction

Where is a story born? From a glance, a word, a voice, a fragment from a sequence of notes that form a melody, a moment, an indelible trace of memory like a snapshot, frozen in time, forever. New York is a city to be read like a book, one containing millions of stories. It becomes known by looking through it, page by page, at each view of the streets, and by knowing how to listen to it. Because New York is not only 'The City of a Thousand Lights,' but also of a thousand voices, with its infinite noises and sounds that provide a soundtrack, like an infinite film. And it is in the particulars, the instants of daily life, which, when assembled with patience and care, form a picture like a jigsaw puzzle. And, it is then that the magic happens, when, from a rebirth, a city is rebuilt. So, why not to listen to all the New York voices and some of the most famous ones?

First of all, New York owes its reputation to the people who made it, here, and, in many ways, made the City itself.

In this book we have gathered together the voices and the stories of people – thinkers, writers, actors, filmmakers and artists – that have given the City a soul, shaping its history, contributing to the rebirth of neighborhoods, as if spreading its image around the world in the fields of the arts and culture, science, cinematography, music, architecture and design.

And so, from their voices you will discover the real New York. New York is a city composed of different microcosms, its neighborhoods, from Harlem to the Upper West Side, from the Upper East Side to Midtown and Downtown, to Greenwich Village, the Lower East Side, the East Village, the Financial District, Chinatown, SoHo, and Tribeca.

Each has its own personality. Each of them is different in a way, but they are all connected to each other as if with an invisible web. They need each other, since they could never exist in isolation. Every human being needs others, as they are all part of a big picture, put together by the same destiny. That is because New York, with all its different faces, is a mirror of humanity itself. And that is because you can either love or hate New York, as no other city in the world. New York is able to reflect you, with bad sides and good sides, light sides and dark sides, like being in a Pirandello play of shadows or in a Dostoevskij drama of life or in a Kafka paradox or in a Tolstoj flow of souls.

Everybody will find himself or herself here, in one way or another, and, like it or not, the feeling will be always intense. No one comes out of New York without being touched. It is impossible not to be involved here, as no other city is so able to get deeply into your blood, to become one with your soul, to let you be astonished by its thousands of lights, by its energy which never sleeps.

New York is also a multitude of colors. What is the color of the City? It is yellow, like its cabs, green, like its parks, red like the hundreds of signs in Times Square or blue, like its sky or the water of its river. It is grey like the metal of its skyscrapers or the concrete of its streets. It is white like the facade of some of its incredible museums and like the clouds racing over your head, following the rhythm of the wind. It is black like the suits of its Wall Street brokers on the sidewalks or of the night, whose dark color contrasts and is interrupted here and there by the millions of colorful lights of the City. They give an abstract feeling, like being in a photograph that is slightly out of focus, where the silhouettes of figures fade away in front of your very eyes, becoming unclear mixtures of form and sensation. It is easy to lose yourself in New York's nights that don't rest until sunrise, holding their own stories, full of life and secrets.

It is easy for the borders between time and space to become blurred when you live in Manhattan. And it is so intense that it is really impossible not to become caught up in all that it is, like the spell of a wonderful magic trick, able to capture your imagination when you least expect it.

The first time I fell in love with New York, was many years ago. I was young, in my twenties, and had just arrived here from Europe, with nothing more than a big dream inside me and an even larger portion of naïvety, that I still like to think I have, despite the many different experiences I have had in the City.

I didn't know anyone here, and I was just a girl with an insane passion and an incredible infatuation with the Big City. I was amazed by how the City looked and, of course, I was fascinated by the tall outlines of the skyscrapers, and the shapes of the marvelous buildings, intersecting with the white clouds above them, as they moved with the wind, in an infinitely blue sky.

I was looking for the New York I knew from the many movies I fell in love with as I grew up, *Breakfast at Tiffany's*, *Barefoot in the Park*, *Bell, Book and Candle*, *Sunday in New York*, *Manhattan*, *Once Upon A Time in America*, *New York, New York* and *Taxi Driver* as well as *Smoke* and other movies that reveal the gritty reality of the City.

What I really loved about New York was the street life, the moments of everyday life, which are indelible memories in my mind, like snapshots in a photo album. I remember them as if they really were scenes in a movie. Because what really makes New York so amazing and beautiful is, primarily, its people – colorful and various, a melting pot of minds, traditions and cultures. Often with that direct, and sometimes aggressive, attitude that makes them real New Yorkers, even though everybody here is a New Yorker when they live in the City.

There are the sounds of the voices – of the many different languages. This is also New York – a small world within a bigger world, all living together. It's a microcosm of tolerance in a modern society, a melting pot of ideas. New York can be a tough interpretation of the American Dream, but it is still the American Dream, where your hopes and dreams can come true, where your talent can get discovered, where everything can change from one moment to the next, where you can reinvent yourself and start again from the beginning.

What is my New York? I am in love with parts of old New York, which probably reminds me of the movies I used to watch when I was a child, in Italy, when I was dreaming, with my big green eyes in my skinny face, of the magic in the Big City. Having lived in Venice – I am from the Veneto on my mother's side – I have learned to appreciate the intimacy of the City that becomes famous and popular, like its stars, to the world. I am in love with those corners of the streets where you still see real New Yorkers rather than tourists.

I am an Uptown person, since I prefer those moments of solitude or the architecture of an old building facing Central Park West, 5th Avenue or Broadway, Park Avenue or some old houses that make Columbus Avenue so special to me. They all remind me of some moments that touched my soul, like notes of melodies, on corners of the Upper West Side and the Upper East Side. If Venice for me, when I used to live there as a student, has always been Vivaldi, my New York has always been Bach in the beauty of the old school Uptown or the jazz of Chet Baker, Charlie Parker, Duke Ellington, Gato Barbieri, or Miles Davis, who used to live on West 77th Street between Riverside and West End Avenue (now called "Miles Davis Way") for nearly 25 years.

I am in love, first of all, with a special section of the neighborhood of the Upper West Side, the one going from West 72nd Street up to around West 96th Street. I have lived in different parts of it, from townhouses to a high-rise condo building, and now I live in an old building on West End Avenue and West 78th Street, in the Historic District of West Collegiate. It is a co-op building, which means that all my neighbors are owners, and some have lived here forever. Most of them are also Jewish and some have amazing stories to tell about how New York used to be. Listening, sometimes to them or to our doormen who have been here many years, colors my mind with other incredible stories of the City. Some of my neighbors are pets, but special pets, also New Yorkers. Lovely and cheeky, sometimes cranky, like real New Yorkers, dogs and cats, and inquisitive parrots. I have recently found out that I have a hawk which might have nested on the roof and which flies, from time to time, to one of the windows facing West End Avenue.

From my bedroom windows, I can see the sailboats on the river reminding me every day of the heritage and connection of New York to the water and of the fact that I live on an island. From here, I discover the pink light of the sunrise or the orange fire of the sunset that paints the water of the river and the clouds of the sky, which, in the winter, evokes in me a remembrance of a romantic German landscape painting of the 19th century by Caspar David Friedrich, inspired by the *Sturm und Drang* movement. My New York is not the one of tall skyscrapers and so, looking out of my window, facing Riverside Park, the trees and old buildings, I can still think I live in a past time.

Our district, West End Collegiate, was named after nearby West End Collegiate Church at West 77th Street and West End Avenue and consists primarily of speculative row houses built in the last 15 years of the 19th century by some of the city's most talented row house architects, including C.P.H. Gilbert, Lamb & Rich and Clarence True. They created blocks with a blend of Italian, French, Flemish Renaissance and other stylistic forms.

I am in love with both Central Park and with its Literary Walk, especially some of the wilder parts of it, where it seems like I'm lost in a forest. I like to go walking, nearly every early morning, by the Hudson River, down at the boathouses dock, or relaxing on a bench, reading a book, on Central Park West facing wonderful

Introduction

residences like The Dakota, where John Lennon, Leonard Bernstein and Lauren Bacall used to live, the Art Deco Century Apartments, The Majestic, The San Remo, The Eldorado, and The Beresford.

Many movies were made in this area and it reminds me a bit of some suggestions in the 1926 *Dream Story* by Arthur Schnitzler, maybe because the characters played by Tom Cruise and Nicole Kidman in *Eyes Wide Shut*, by Stanley Kubrick, loosely based upon the novella, live right in an apartment on Central Park West. In the same way, I adore walking around the old houses of Gramercy Park, a small fenced-in private historic park open only to the residents who live in the beautiful buildings around it. I go to Pete's Tavern around there, or to a romantic and discreet historical spot called The Inn at Irving Place, in two townhouses built in 1834 that are more like a home than a hotel.

I indulge in the familiarity of Café Lalo or Café Luxembourg or even Lansky's diner or the tiny gastronomic location of Zabar's where people all sit at the same table or at a small window facing the street. My favorite coffee places are Caffe Reggio close to Washington Square Park in Greenwich Village, or Café Sabarsky, in the Neue Galerie, for coffee and cake. A restaurant I used to be in love with is the old Café des Artistes. I sometimes still go to the renovated one, mostly to admire the murals of Howard Chandler Christy, which are still there. The original restaurant first opened in 1917 and was designed for the residents of the Hotel des Artistes, since the apartments lacked kitchens, and where artists like Marcel Duchamp, Norman Rockwell, Isadora Duncan and Rudolph Valen-

tino lived. As for hotels, I find the Hotel Carlyle really a wonderful place for its history and the music of Café Carlyle, which makes it an even more special place. Another amazing hotel, the whole year, but especially for Christmas, when you can see it even from 5th Avenue, is The Peninsula Hotel. It is also an institution and history of New York, with a wonderful bar on the rooftop overlooking all the City.

As a European, I am fascinated by the historical clubs of old school New York like The Metropolitan, The National Arts Club, The Players, The Explorers Club, and the Friars Club. You must be a member to go there (and sometimes even that is difficult, as they have a tradition of passing membership from family to family), but you can also take part in some events or exhibitions which they sometimes open to the public.

And what I really do adore about the City is looking at it from the sky. It can be in a helicopter, which I use in my work as a professional photographer and from where New York looks like a puzzle of different sensations and colors. Or it can be from the tall skyscrapers like the Empire State Building, where I like to go around midnight sometimes, just to admire the lights like King Kong did, or Rockefeller Center. Nothing takes my breath away more than the moment just after the sunset when the sky over the west seems to be on fire with marvelous shades of red, pink and violet. I always come here and look, when I want to feel in love, again and again, with New York.

A group yoga lesson held in **Times Square**.

WOODY ALLEN

The "Mind" of the City

In his world, there is no reason why some things happen and others don't. Everything is possible, whatever works. This is how New York City thinks, its way of life. There's no one way of doing anything, except how it's done here.

No one knows New York City like Woody Allen, who probes its depths, wandering deep into obscure corners, absorbing each hidden neighborhood, its culture, music and urban art. He is 'one of them', and at the same time, their voyeur. He is both inside Manhattan and outside Manhattan, looking with the eye of a director, the mind of a genius, the sensibility of an actor, the creativity and the curiosity of a writer.

For one of his most famous movies, *New York Stories* (1989), Allen teamed up with Martin Scorsese and Francis Ford Coppola to create an anthology about New Yorkers. When he tells a story, Woody Allen takes it beyond the individual lives of New Yorkers, to something larger about human nature. His stories penetrate not only into the heart of the City's middle-class and its wealthiest residents, but also take a particular interest in those who are not so lucky.

"I grew up in Brooklyn in the lower class," says Woody Allen. "I still feel these are my roots even though I moved to Manhattan when I was only 19 years old, found work, got married, and developed a circle of friends, some of which had very good jobs," he recalls. "I learned to get to know the different levels of society in New York. I had friends who made money, even a lot of money, yet that didn't prevent them from making tremendous fools of themselves and ending up with tragic lives, like Cate Blanchett's character in *Blue Jasmine* (2013)."

He is not afraid to uncover that darker side of human nature that is in every one of us, the side that we would rather not see, or would like to forget. With incredible intelligence, talent and an endless love for the City, Allen explores this darkness with an ironic and original spirit. His prodigious imagination produces work that can cleverly trick and entertain, like a magician who not only makes us laugh, but makes us think as well.

In the end, what is the meaning of life? What is the soul of "The City of a Thousand Lights?" Is New York able to love, suffer, feel and struggle like a human being? When you watch Woody Allen's movies, it's as if Manhattan is able to breath, listen, taste and smell. It's as if the City is a person with a special sixth sense, an almost intuitive, surreal, even shamanic sense that we can barely perceive. We cannot see or touch this invisible essence, but it happens all around us.

> I love the City in an emotional, irrational way, like loving your mother and your father even though they are drunks or thieves.

> "Life is so much about luck.
> I would say at least ninety-nine per cent,
> especially in New York,
> sometimes people are frightened to admit it."

We can only experience it, as in his film *The Curse of the Jade Scorpion* (2001).

In Allen's world, everything is about this mysterious sense of New York, about taking a chance, and being in the right place at the right time. "Life is so much about luck. I would say at least ninety-nine per cent, especially in New York," he declares. "Sometimes people are frightened to admit it. They want to think that they are in control of their lives, but that's not true," he says.

"Americans like to think of themselves as having made their own luck. They keep on thinking this so they can believe they are in control, but they aren't. None of us are."

Where is this luck? "Everywhere in the City and anywhere in the world," says Allen. "It can be the luck of the genes, the luck of the draw, or the luck of what happens during the day. It can be the luck of not being there when the bomb goes off on the other guy's bus, or the plane you didn't take that crashes, or of being born one place instead of another, or even the luck that may be waiting for you around a street corner."

Woody Allen is "the Mind" of New York City. Simultaneously, he psychoanalyses his characters and himself. He explores the thoughts, feelings and expectations, the hopes and dreams of the City and its residents.

Like the City itself, he is with them when they fall in love, when they cry, when they feel the sweetness and bitterness of life. He is part of the light and shadow of "The City That Never Sleeps."

Like an army of laboring ants, New York stories are always active in his mind. They exist as if in a Pirandello drama, fighting to be brought to life. When they are born into the real world, that's when the problems begin. "I feel like the only way to make it through life is distraction," Allen explains. "You can distract yourself in a million ways – reading a book, writing a script, watching television or a movie, listening to music, or watching a soccer game. Or, you can create problems like a lot of New Yorkers do in order to survive, even though they know at the end of the day, these aren't life or death problems," he adds. "They can be solved one way or another."

Woody Allen is like a New York dream that came true. An entirely self-made man, he was born Allen Stewart Konigsberg, in the Bronx, and was raised in a Jewish family in Brooklyn. His mother Nettie was a bookkeeper at her family's delicatessen, and Martin, his father, was a jewelry engraver and waiter. Allen's grandparents came from Russia and Austria. By heritage, he is an Ashkenazi Jew.

Reinventing himself as Woody Allen, the intellectual atheist of the Upper East Side, the filmmaker at first wrote jokes and worked as a comedian, making his debut at the legendary *Duplex* club in Greenwich Village, before becoming a star in the movie industry. All he did was be himself, a unique, strong and charismatic personality.

A panoramic aerial view of **Times Square.**

"I am always surprised
when anyone wants to hear authentic jazz."

Like a character in one of his movies, Woody Allen is a larger-than-life man, a vibrant icon of American pop culture. New York would not be the same without him.

Even if recently he has been traveling the world to film in the different cities that have charmed him – London for *Match Point* (2005); Paris for *Midnight in Paris* (2011); Barcelona for *Vicky Cristina Barcelona* (2008); San Francisco for *Blue Jasmine* (2013); and Rome for *To Rome with Love* (2012) – he admits that when he's away, he misses the City. He always comes back.

An artist of many talents, Allen also loves theater and jazz. He writes plays for Broadway and every Monday night he plays clarinet with his band, the New Orleans Jazz Band, at the Carlyle Hotel's Café Carlyle nightclub on the Upper East Side. The nightclub, an icon in the City music scene, is packed every time he plays. "I am always surprised when anyone wants to hear authentic jazz," he muses.

"There are a million things to do in New York, a million stories to tell, a million great locations in the city," says Allen. "I have done many movies here, and I will keep on doing them. I don't think I have even scratched the surface of New York City." What does he miss most when he is away? "That I am not going to be able to see any baseball," he answers. "That's a big loss for me."

To see into Woody Allen's New York City, all you have to do is follow his stories.

There are so many New York locations in his productions. For Allen, it all begins and ends at home. "It's nice to work at home. I like that, to have my own shower, my own bed, my own house," he says.

Authentic jazz
Woody Allen plays the clarinet with the Eddy Davis New Orleans Jazz Band at the Carlyle Hotel's Café Carlyle.

After keeping the same one bedroom apartment for many years, he now lives with his whole family on the Upper East Side of Manhattan.

"Even if I grew up in Brooklyn, my concept of New York is the Manhattan that I knew from Hollywood movies, a city ablaze with lights, with champagne corks popping, and a gorgeous woman coming home at 4 o'clock in the morning with an ermine wrap draped over her shoulders," he muses. "We didn't live like that in Brooklyn. When I think of the New York I dreamt about as a child, it was not as realistic or accurate as those portrayed in Spike Lee's or Martin Scorsese's movies."

We discover Allen's portraits of the City in movies such as *Manhattan* (1979); *Hannah and Her Sisters* (1986); *Crimes and Misdemeanors* (1989), where he combines tragic and comic elements; *Annie Hall* (1977); *Broadway Danny Rose* (1984), where he plays a New York show business agent; *Radio Days* (1987), a film about his childhood in Brooklyn; *Husbands and Wives* (1992); *Manhattan Murder Mystery* (1993); *Bullets Over Broadway* (1994); the musical *Everyone Says I Love You* (1996); *Small Time Crooks* (2000) and others.

In The Paris Theater, which is seen in *Annie Hall* (1977), you can still see great movies. At the Riverview Terrace at 59th Street and FDR Drive, you can still watch the sunrise like Allen and Keaton did in *Manhattan* (1979) from one of the benches along the river, looking out to a view of the Queensboro Bridge. The 21 Club is a historic restaurant, where the characters in *Manhattan Murder Mystery* (1993) had dinner.

21 Club
The facade of this historic restaurant, which was a speakeasy in the Prohibition era. The lawn jockey statuettes were donated by the establishment's most prestigious clients. Woody Allen shot a scene of his *Manhattan Murder Mystery* here.

The **Dean & DeLuca Cafe** in SoHo.

Allen loves the Russian Tea Room ("I have long been a regular at this uptown spot"), one of the most famous tearooms in the world.

The romantic Cherry Lane Theatre, seen in *Another Woman* (1988), was founded by poet Edna St. Vincent Millay in 1924, and frequented by well-known and emerging artists. It's where James Dean used to work. It's still a famous and popular Off-Broadway spot, and close to the old Grange Hall restaurant (today called Commerce), at 50 Commerce Street, which featured in *Anything Else* (2003).

The little house in the Village, at number 100, is where Woody Allen and Mia Farrow walk in *Hannah and Her Sisters* (1986), while number 75 and 1/2 is the narrowest house, built in 1873, where the actor John Barrymore and the poet Edna St. Vincent Millay lived. At 278 Bleecker Street, in a lively area, is John's Pizzeria, a staple of the West Village since 1929. These are the streets of the Village, the Greenwich Village of poets, writers, and artists such as Jackson Pollock, and the Beat generation, that run like a dream through the imagination. Other recognizable New York landmarks in Allen's movies are Dean & DeLuca, an elegant gourmet food market at 560 Broadway, in the heart of SoHo, where Mia Farrow goes in *Husbands and Wives* (1992); Nom Wah Tea Parlor, the

Husbands and Wives
The counter at the Dean & DeLuca Cafe in SoHo is always a very lively place. It was the location for one scene of Woody Allen's 1992 movie starring Mia Farrow and Judy Davis.

The **Metropolitan Museum of Art**.

"I've loved the City my whole life. To me it's like a great woman."

first dim sum restaurant in New York, in *Radio Days* (1987); Lanza's, a famous Italian eatery, where an important scene takes place in *Manhattan Murder Mystery* (1993), and Yonah Schimmel Knish Bakery, the old school knishery, which the character Larry David hits up in *Whatever Works* (2009).

Woody Allen's Manhattan is revealed to us through the moments of New York street life depicted in his films. These beautiful pictures hang in a fictional museum of abstract memories and follow the City's history from the 1970s through today. Among the famous places are the Pomander Walk (260-266 West 94th Street); The Metropolitan Museum of Art ("I am a long time fan of it"); Hayden Planetarium; Guggenheim Museum, where Allen has a memorable scene with Diane Keaton in *Manhattan* (1979); the Whitney Museum of American Art; Central Park Zoo ("The only place where you can see penguins in the middle of New York City!"); and the toy store FAO Schwarz ("which you can see in *Mighty Aphrodite* (1995)").

Guggenheim Museum
Frank Lloyd Wright's spiral ramp gallery in the Guggenheim Museum was immortalized in Allen's film *Manhattan* (1979).

Through Allen's movies you discover secret windows into the City's history and culture, into the thousands of beautiful faces that make up the melting pot of Manhattan. "New York is like Calcutta," Woody says. "I love the City in an emotional, irrational way, like loving your mother and your father even though they are drunks or thieves."

"I've loved the City my whole life," Woody Allen declares. "To me it's like a great woman."

To Allen, New York is magic, like filmmaking. "When I was young and still at school, I ran away from my problems to the cinema," he recalls. "Today, I run away from them behind the camera, where I get to meet the most beautiful women in the world like Diane Keaton, Marion Cotillard, Rachel McAdams, Carla Bruni, Penelope Cruz, Scarlett Johansson, and Cate Blanchett."

"I believe that a bit of magic can save humanity from its dilemma, and New York is full of it," says Woody Allen.

The City That Never Sleeps

New York becomes even more special at night, when it almost seems to be blanketed by thousands of lights. This is a panoramic view of Downtown and the Freedom Tower from the Empire State Building terrace.

The new **Whitney Museum of American Art**, designed by Renzo Piano.

LIDIA BASTIANICH

The "Culinary Queen" of the City

Lidia Bastianich has become a great and beloved culinary star in New York, due to her warmth, her Italian sense of hospitality and her deliciously authentic Italian flavors. She is also a symbol of the New York American Dream.

She was born in Pula, Istria (now part of Croatia), in 1947, a part of Italy that had been given to the newly formed communist Yugoslavia after World War II. "Because of Tito's Communist regime, my parents decided that we needed to leave. In 1956, my father, Vittorio, sent my mother, myself and my brother, Franco, to visit relatives in Trieste, Italy. My father remained in Pula as the regime insisted that one member of the family stay to ensure that the rest of the family would return. However, two weeks later, my father escaped and crossed the border into Italy. After staying with our extended family for a few months, we ended up becoming residents of San Sabba, a political refugee camp. We were part of the largest Istrian exodus in history."

Approximately two years later, Lidia's family was granted the opportunity to emigrate to the United States and they arrived in New York. "I remember landing at what is now JFK Airport, and taking the bus into Manhattan.

> New York allows me to take a journey all around the world and experience different cultures in only a few hours.

"The skyscrapers and bridges were simply amazing, like nothing I had ever seen before." Lidia's family stayed in a hotel until they moved, for a short period, to North Bergen, New Jersey. Soon afterwards, the family found distant relatives in Astoria, Queens and they moved there. "When I arrived in Astoria, there were many Italian and German immigrants. In fact, when I was only fourteen years old, I began working in a bakery owned by Christopher Walken's father. Although I started at the counter, I found myself gravitating towards the kitchen whenever there was a chance. I loved decorating the cakes and desserts," says Lidia.

Astoria is an area that Lidia still visits although the demographics have changed as many Indian, Egyptian and Asian immigrants have arrived and made the area their home.

After Lidia graduated from high school, and while going to college, she began to work in local Italian restaurants. It was during this period that she also met her future husband and restaurateur, Felice Bastianich, also from Istria. They married in 1966 and had two children, Joseph and Tanya. They opened their first restaurant, Buonavia in Forest Hills, Queens, just before Tanya was born.

The **Statue of Liberty,** the symbol of the **American Dream.**

> "I always feel great emotion when I see the Statue of Liberty; it reminds me of when I arrived as an immigrant and, more importantly, how lucky I am to have arrived in this great city and country."

Although Lidia started at the front of the house, she and Felice hired the best Italian-American chef that they could find, to run the kitchen. She learned the Italian-American classics alongside him while also introducing him to the flavors that she recalled from spending time with her grandmother in Istria. "We were serving veal scaloppine but I was also showing him how to make dishes like *risi e bisi, jota,* and *palacinke.*"

Buonavia was an immediate success and several years later Lidia and Felice opened a second restaurant in Queens. But it was in 1981 that they made their big decision to move to Manhattan and open the flagship restaurant, Felidia, where Lidia became the chef. Felidia received three stars from the 'New York Times' soon after it opened and has earned three further stars since.

In the 1990s, Lidia was blessed when her children also decided to join the business. Joe, after a brief stint on Wall Street, traveled through Italy and opened a theater district Italian eatery with her in 1993. He then collaborated with Mario Batali, years later, on several projects and has since collaborated on a number of projects with Mario and Lidia, including Esca, Del Posto and Eataly New York and Eataly Chicago.

"New York is a place where my family was able to start again;
it's a world of thousands of possibilities and hopes."

The main hall of the former Immigrant Inspection Station at **Ellis Island**.
Old trunks left by immigrants, now on display at the **Ellis Island Immigration Museum**.

It is at Eataly where Lidia offers culinary classes as Dean of La Scuola (The School). Tanya, Lidia's daughter, earned her doctorate in Art History at Oxford and then began collaborating with Lidia on her television shows and cookbooks as well as some of the restaurants. She is currently developing additional culinary television programs as part of Tavola Productions, which she runs with her mother.

Lidia's mother, Erminia, still lives with Lidia and helps to maintain the large vegetable garden, produce from which Lidia still uses in her recipes at home and sometimes even at the restaurants. She also appears in several epi-

sodes of 'Lidia's Kitchen', the PBS TV show, and, of course, loves to have her great-grandchildren over for visits.

New York represented a new beginning and a new home for Lidia Bastianich and, when asked how she feels about other landmarks like the Statue of Liberty or Ellis Island, her response is simple. "I always feel great emotion when I see those two symbols of New York; it reminds me of when I arrived as an immigrant and, more importantly, how lucky I am to have arrived in this great city and country. New York is a place where my family was able to start again; it's a world of thousands of possibilities and hopes," she says.

"I like going for a walk in Central Park.
Not only is it incredibly beautiful with its baseball fields,
green lawns, and lakes but it also has an energy
that simply makes me feel alive."

Central Park illuminated by the street lamps.
The fountain at **Bethesda Terrace** in Central Park.

"I love New York; it's my home. Sometimes I feel that I need a break from this bustling city and my travel schedule allows me to accomplish that, but I always feel the need to come back as it's where I belong," says Lidia. "New York is a city of constant change, whether you are in Manhattan, Queens, or any of the other boroughs. I adore Broadway in Astoria where many Italian and Greek Americans have their residences and businesses but I also love the cafés of Greenwich Village, SoHo and the East Village." Lidia stresses that New York still feels like the most exciting place in the world to her. "New York allows me to take a journey all around the world and experience different cultures in only a few hours. There is an energy that I feel as I go from place to place; it's part of my soul as I watch the people walking, the cars and taxis buzzing around the streets, and the unexpected aromas and flavors of different ethnic foods wafting from the street food vendors. I can always find a great quick meal on the go."

Lidia is a big fan of the parks of New York. "I like going for a walk in Central Park. Not only is it incredibly beautiful with its baseball fields, green lawns, and lakes but it also has an energy that simply makes me feel alive."

She also admires the small park facing the East River close to the United Nations Headquarters, as she loves watching the boats going up and down the East River.

Bryant Park is also a favorite, especially at Christmas as she watches families and friends on the ice rink in the winter and performing artists in the summer. "I feel really close to Astoria Park, where I often watch people playing soccer like they do in Italy, under the great Triborough Bridge."

Skyscrapers have always fascinated Lidia since her arrival in the city as a young girl. "I particularly love the Chrysler Building; it was always the ultimate symbol of New York for me. I have always been amazed by its Art Deco design, and I still love driving into Manhattan from Queens as the sun sets behind the skyscrapers, creating futuristic

The **Lincoln Center for the Perfoming Arts**.

effects. The skyline continues to evoke emotions in me each time I see it, even if I have seen it thousands of times." Lidia has inherited a great passion for classical music and the opera, due to her Italian roots.

It's no surprise that she has a great fondness for The Lincoln Center for the Performing Arts, which includes twenty outdoor and indoor performance facilities, including The Alice Tully Hall, a renowned concert hall that offers prestigious programs in dance, drama and music, and the Avery Fisher Hall, home of the New York Philharmonic, the Metropolitan Opera House and the David H. Koch Theater, home of the New York City Ballet.

"I love the Lincoln Center, its theaters, its beautiful central fountain, used as a meeting point for so many here.

"It's an incredible center for the arts with classical music, plays, ballets and marvelous concerts."

As for museums, one of Lidia's favorites is the MoMA, the Museum of Modern Art. She is also thrilled to see that in Queens there is a great Renaissance of Art and Film happening at the moment. In fact, there is MoMA PS1, an affiliate of MoMA, in Long Island, that she is proud to talk about. "The Kaufman Astoria Studios have never been so active and productive," she explains.

In the end, Lidia admits that her deep connection to New York is still through its food. "For me, New York City is a melting pot and when I am in the mood for Asian cuisine, especially Korean, my thoughts go right to Main Street in Flushing, Queens." She has recently become very interested in Korean eateries, which are very popular along this street. "The food is delicious, the owners passionate and the New York energy that I love is here."

Lidia knows that with time Flushing's Main Street will probably change yet again as another immigrant population moves in. "Everything in New York City is continuously changing, evolving and ultimately surprising me, inspiring me to do something that I might never have thought would be possible. And that's what I love about New York City."

Classical Ballet
Ballet dancers of the New York City Ballet performing *The Nutcracker* visit the floor of the New York Stock Exchange.

MARIO BATALI

The "Chef" of the City

Like a master painter, he has "painted" New York with his orange touch and made it fall in love with Italy. Iconic orange Crocs aside (though he wears them even on the red carpet), Mario Batali is, above all, the greatest chef in the City. "New York is rich in different flavors, spices, and colors, and is classic, modern, and experimental all at once," he says.

Joyful and playful, like a modern-day Bacchus, you can "breathe" this atmosphere at Eataly NYC, the artisanal Italian food and wine marketplace Batali opened with Lidia and Joe Bastianich and Adam and Alex Saper, an international initiative of entrepreneur Oscar Farinetti. "It offers a selection of restaurants where you can sample many kinds of meat, fish and pasta dishes and on the roof sits a fashionable Birreria. This is a true culinary temple for Italy fans, where countless regional and local products can be found."

"I wanted to make New Yorkers know the sense of 'la dolce vita' and its flavors. In the end New York is a place where you can experiment and play with tastes, taking a little from all over the world. If you don't take a risk in New York, where can you do it? I feel so creative here. You can challenge people to react much more than anywhere else.

> New York is rich in different flavors, spices, and colors, and is classic, modern, and experimental all at once.

"New York is a real gastronomic melting pot universe, where a dish can be creative and beautiful, like a piece of art."

Batali has also made food interesting to New Yorkers through his TV shows and many books. Among them are *Molto Italiano: 327 Simple Italian Recipes to Cook at Home (Ecco 2005)*; the *New York Times* Bestseller *Mario Batali Italian Grill (Ecco 2008)*; and *Molto Batali: Simple Family Meals from My Home to Yours (Ecco 2011)*.

He has taught New Yorkers to appreciate the art of cooking, and shopping for food. "New York is a paradise for 'gastronomic shopping'. I like going to the local farmers' markets in town. You can find fresh and seasonal products and a lot of them are easy to cook, like beans, tomatoes, lentils, peas, extra virgin olive oil, balsamic vinegar, pumpkin, bread crumbs, and many spices like chipotle, chorizo, chili. In New York, you can find products from all over the world. There is always something fascinating to create and bring to the table. In a restaurant, like in the fashion world, you can launch a trend," says the Chef.

For Batali, cooking is a way of living in many nuances, from the most casual to the traditional to the eccentric and unique. And, he has masterfully brought this understanding to New Yorkers.

He is an expert in the history and culture of Italian cuisine, which influences his way of living and eating, his family values and traditional culture.

"My feeling for cuisine can be experienced in my New York restaurants, which give a sense of the City, rustic and simple, elegant and trendy, each one different, each one incorporating a bit of my personality. You want to get to know Mario? Just eat with me!" he laughs.

So, his New York, as Batali says, "can combine the elegance of an Italian enoteca with the fun bustle of a crowded Italian train station." This is the Otto Enoteca Pizzeria. Or, it can be the glamour of "an exuberant celebration of the best of Italian food, wine and lifestyle," at Babbo Ristorante e Enoteca, where many celebrities go.

In his vision, New York can be elegant, like Del Posto. "This is an elegant Italian restaurant with the ambiance of European luxury," he explains. "In New York you can also discover the rustic roots of the regional heritage of many of its people," he points out, thinking of Lupa Osteria Romana. "It is a Roman trattoria serving Roman dishes with a New York balance, and like the City, able to melt together different styles."

New York is a city on the water, and Esca celebrates this. "It is a southern Italian trattoria devoted to celebrating the fruits of the sea."

Latinos are a huge community in New York City and Batali has always been fascinated by the warm flavor of Spanish cuisine. So, he has contributed to the creation of Bar Jamón, a casual tapas-style place, and Casa Mono. "Here you open the door, and it looks like you could be in Spain, even if you still breathe the metropolitan air. You can find 'raciones' of Catalan specialties and dishes from all corners of the Iberian Peninsula. And you can taste them with a New York style cocktail, if you want, rather than with a glass of excellent wine".

Gastronomic Creativity and Culture
The entrance of EATALY, a delicatessen, restaurant and beer hall co-founded and created by Mario Batali located on the corner of 23rd Street and 5th Avenue.

A delicatessen counter at **EATALY**.

Products of **traditional Italian cuisine** can be purchased at EATALY.

"I wanted to make New Yorkers know the sense of 'la dolce vita' and its flavors."

Although he now feels like a real New Yorker, Batali was born in Seattle, Washington. His father, Armando Batali, was of Italian ancestry, while his mother was of French-Canadian and English descent. "I lived in Italy for a while and I love it, I love its widely varied regional and local gastronomy," he shares. "I also lived in Spain for a while, but in the end I feel most of all like an American, as it's here that I grew up. I also have a house in Michigan where I like to go to relax and spend time every summer."

Batali believes "family is the most important thing in life," and always wishes to have more time to spend with them. So, not surprisingly, all of Batali's family members are part of the business. His wife, Susi, has supported him from the start and knows plenty about food and produce. His two sons, Leo and Benno, make him proud with their love of cooking, and together have published *The Batali Brothers Cookbook (Ecco 2013)*, a selection of their own and their father's simple recipes.

As a man who made it all by himself, Batali is very much a part of the New York American Dream and with his whole family he also shares an immense love for the City. While at college he worked as a dishwasher, then as a pizza maker and cook around America and all over Europe. By twenty-seven, though, he was already a highly paid young chef.

YOU ARE
WHAT YOU
EATALY

"New York is not a City where people like to cook at home. Most New Yorkers like to eat out and go to restaurants. I still like cooking at home for the whole family," he enthuses.

"These days my kids take over from me in the kitchen when I'm not there, and they're asking questions about ingredients, cooking time and preparation. It's nice to see a tradition continue, and to see that they have the same great passion as me for the City."

For him the New York of today is the art of sharing with the people you love, not just at the table but generally in life.

"For me, New York is the comfort of those places that, when you see them, remind you how beautiful it is and why you love it so much. My family and I love Washington Square. Just going to the park and watching people perform and play live music. We love Union Square, where we all go to the Greenmarket. It's so much fun to go shopping together. Another favorite for us is Smorgasburg and Brooklyn Flea and Food Market on the Williamsburg waterfront, where you can eat, shop, walk and visit all the vendors. The sense of all being together to share, which is also New York."

And, for him there are iconic places that make you feel alive, every time you step into them. "I am fascinated by the Brooklyn Bridge, where I go walking with the kids. The view from there, above it all, the water, being suspended in the air gives you a feel for the City, a picture of its amazing beauty and greatness, with the outline of the Lower Manhattan skyscrapers soaring into the sky, of the possibilities and chances you can take here. It makes you think that, if what you see in front of your eyes is possible, then everything you can imagine is possible!" he reflects.

Farmers' Markets
The various markets offering fruit, vegetables and delicatessen products are very popular in New York City. The one seen here, in Union Square, is one of Mario Batali's favorites.

"In New York, you can find products
from all over the world. There is always something
fascinating to create and bring to the table."

"For me, New York is the comfort of those places that,
when you see them, remind you how beautiful
it is and why you love it so much."

The **Brooklyn flea market** in winter is held in the Williamsburgh Savings Bank Building.
The Manhattan skyline, viewed from **Brooklyn Bridge**.

"I try to go there at least once a month. It reminds me why I love the City so much. With the same emotions in my heart I take the Staten Island Ferry, to admire its wonderful view of the Statue of Liberty. And every time is like the first time. I realize how I'm still deeply in love with New York. Each time I go away for a while, like to Lake Michigan, where we have a house, I come back here, and I love it even more. New York is just such a special place to be."

As a great humanitarian and philanthropist, Batali is also an example for New York City: in 2008, he created the Mario Batali Foundation.

"New York is a place with a strong sense of community, and has thrived largely because of this. As a father, I wanted to educate and empower children in difficulty. The Foundation organizes many events to raise funds for research into child diseases, children's literacy and hunger relief and, with the Food Bank initiative, we want to guarantee food to all New Yorkers," Batali says.

"Poverty is, unfortunately, still a 'face' of New York. There are still too many families in the City who live in poverty, and we must do our best to help them. Helping each other to make it, being a part of it: this is also what New York is."

CANDACE BUSHNELL

The "Glamour" of the City

Blonde, blue-eyed, lean, sophisticated, and beautiful, Candace Bushnell has a gift for tapping into the zeitgeist of New York. The best-selling author personifies the glamour of the City that she so marvelously portrays in her novels. Depicted on TV and in movies, like the hugely successful *Sex and the City*, or *Lipstick Jungle*, *The Carrie Diaries*, and *Summer and the City*, Bushnell's New York is sexy, elegant and stunning.

"The intense red lipstick and the fresh scent of just blow-dried hair, the magical glimpse of cool eyes under black mascara, the feline walk of a lady on 5th Avenue. That is also New York," she says.

And her New York wants to have fun. "New York is playful, casual and amazing but it's also romantic, and wants to fall in love. The City opens like a Chinese box. You can move from one space to another, from one page to another, discovering its secrets and peculiarities."

Born in Glastonbury, Connecticut, Candace Bushnell attended Rice University and New York University. She moved to New York when she was only 19 years old, and started living in Greenwich Village. Her early life resembles that of her most famous character, Carrie Bradshaw, as depicted in *The Carrie Diaries*, a prequel to *Sex and the City*.

> New York is playful, casual and amazing but it's also romantic, and wants to fall in love.

Like many New Yorkers, choosing to divide their lives between the country and the city, Bushnell also has a home in Roxbury, Connecticut, with her dogs and a horse that she adores.

"I love horseback riding now, and, of course, I do that fashionably too," says Candace. "I've always been a socialite and I still like going to parties, though a bit less than when I used to go to Studio 54. New York is a beautiful City, but like a lover who's always demanding something, it does not give you a break. It can become an obsession, so it's nice to take a break."

"Now, I spend a lot of time in Connecticut, even though I'm sure I would miss New York desperately if I never came. You can hate or love New York, but you can't live without it. Especially after it gets into your blood and becomes a part of you."

Bushnell loves Greenwich Village. "When I moved to the neighborhood it wasn't as nice as it is now," she explains. "I liked that there were so many shops and it was so cozy, like a real village. Some of them have still survived globalization, and today I still like to go shopping for porcelain and antiques in small street markets as much as in designer stores like ABC in SoHo," she says. "But it's in the small shops, where you know the owner, that you can discover the soul of the intimate New York."

"You can hate or love New York, but you can't live without it.
Especially after it gets into your blood
and becomes a part of you."

Christmas trees and lights decorate the **Pulitzer Fountain**.
The GE Building at **Rockefeller Center**.

WISDOM AND ★ KNOWLEDGE ★ SHALL BE THE ★ STABILITY OF THY TIMES

"New York is a beautiful City,
but like a lover who's always demanding something,
it does not give you a break."

Candace loves the side of the City that only a real New Yorker knows. It's the side of New York that takes time to get to know, and which most tourists will miss. "It's this 'village' face I like most in New York, the fact that you are in a big city, but can feel like you live in a small village," she muses. "But ultimately, it has been tough to make it in New York. New York, as beautiful as it can be, is still a tough place and it will never change in that sense."

Bushnell worked as a writer and journalist in New York for years before becoming famous for her 1994 "Sex and the City" column in the *The New York Observer*. Candace's column was inspired by her own, and her friends', romantic experiences with men in Manhattan. "New York is also this: dating, going out, meeting people, and, why not... let's say it... having sex – a lot of sex. New York can be fun, but also incredibly hard when you don't have money."

Christmas at Rockefeller Center

The very tall illuminated tree and the ice skating rink at Rockefeller Center are two images that embody Christmas in New York.

"The City opens like a Chinese box. You can move from one space to another, from one page to another, discovering its secrets and peculiarities."

She remembers how she started in New York. "I was not rich and I had to fight and work hard to make it," she says. "I lived with different roommates in many different apartments. Like all New Yorkers, for a variety of reasons, I have moved continuously. Once, we were four girls in the same apartment. Me and three actresses, and two of those worked on Broadway. They practiced their roles and sang the whole day, so I ended up learning all the words of the musicals they had to play!"

In those days, Bushnell liked to hang out in places like the Bowery Bar and Moomba, which has since closed. "There was a lot of freedom in New York when I moved here," she recalls. "I have always loved this about the City, but now, with modern technology, it's changed. Back then, people didn't have cell phones, and they couldn't just take a photo and put it on Facebook or Twitter. There was a special privacy in New York that doesn't exist any more."

Luxury on Display
A dazzling high fashion shop window, arranged for the Christmas season, at one of the most exclusive luxury item stores on 5th Avenue.

Street Art in SoHo
SoHo is the neighborhood of creative fashion, shopping, design and art. In this photograph an artist is exhibiting and selling his works on the street.

"New York is a City of bars and cocktails and crazy nights out.
I hope it can hang on to that romance you still see
in movies sometimes, and that it will never lose it!"

As an expert in relationships, and, after so many books and so much research on the topic, deeply familiar with New York society, Candace Bushnell finds that the City has evolved even in that sense. "Relationships between men and women have changed in the City," she reflects. "I believe that the Internet has ruined everything a little bit. It's taken away the poetry, romance and even the adventure. Now, a lot of people meet on one of these dating websites, where you fill out your profile as if you were going shopping at the supermarket. I found it a little sad."

"I don't know..." Bushnell says, "It seems to me that we had so much more fun before, when my girls and I went out to bars or to a nightclub to enjoy a Cosmopolitan. New Yorkers still do it, but the digital revolution has certainly changed things."

"New York is a City of bars and cocktails and crazy nights out," says Candace, "I hope it can hang on to that romance you still see in movies sometimes, and that it will never lose it!"

Her advice regarding New York? "Spend more time working on yourself and on your career than worrying too much about men. And then The City will 'smile' on you."

The **Meatpacking District.**

Gigantic billboard in the newly revived Meatpacking District.

ROBERT DE NIRO

The "Sculptor" of the City

Like a sculptor using his bare hands to reshape the lifeless concrete of the streets, Robert De Niro has transformed a gray landscape into a shining work of art. His creative spark ignites a thousand emotions and illuminates the faces in a history of Manhattan's melting pot. This grand patron of the City has converted a pocket of sidewalks and worn buildings into the thriving Tribeca that we know today.

De Niro, one of the film world's best actors, directors, producers and entrepreneurs, has watched New York change every fraction of a second, in a surreal kaleidoscope of vibrant, interlocking patterns and dissonant, colorful rhythms. It takes only a moment to recognize one of his characters as he walks along a New York street, immersed in the irrevocable memories that flicker between the old brownstones. His characters possess a kind of poignancy. They convey an experience that is imprinted on us like a snapshot, suspended in the pale dusk of a winter's day.

Robert De Niro's entire life is a love letter to New York. He has become a "king" of the City, part of its history and evolution, and an embodiment of its resilient spirit. There are men who love action more than words. There are men who not only aspire to dream, but who, with laser focus and stunning talent, know how to transform their dream into reality. Even as he looks away, De Niro's eyes cast this depth and vision as they reach effortlessly into the human soul. He has that chameleonic quality of his film characters that, just like him, have become a legendary part of our collective imagination.

"New York forgives nothing. Yet, it's a place that grows inside you, and with you, until it is in your blood. In New York, talent matters, but it's not enough," declares De Niro. "It is our choices that determine whether that talent will rise or not. In New York, even if you have talent, there is the risk of not going anywhere."

De Niro has been able to reach the essence of New York City, as if it were a woman's body and he an attentive lover, gradually exploring and getting to know her secrets with the seductive power of conquest. What does he most like about New York? "I find that in my City, I can feel infinite moments and universes, a richness of cultures like no place else in the world," he shares. "New York represents, first of all, my home. There are times when I find I am willing to stay at home, feeling the need to spend time with my family. And there are times, when, as one of the most beautiful cities in the world, New York beckons to me to explore.

> I find that in my City,
> I can feel infinite moments
> and universes, a richness
> of cultures like no place
> else in the world.

"New York forgives nothing. Yet, it's a place that grows
inside you, and with you, until it is in your blood."

"There is no other place where you feel this same energy, this pulse of life," says De Niro. "New York is contagious. More and more I feel here that I don't want to miss a single moment."

Perched in an apartment window in Greenwich Village, one of De Niro's first characters, Rubin, spies on the daily activities of New York City life in Brian De Palma's black comedy *Hi, Mom!* (1970).

Throughout his career, De Niro has appeared in some of the greatest American movies and worked with some of its most talented directors. It was beside Martin Scorsese, another "king" of New York, that De Niro developed his instinct for the City. "I am very grateful to Scorsese," says De Niro, "because he has been a true mentor. I hope I will always be able to work with him on new projects."

In *Mean Streets* (1973), De Niro became immersed in Little Italy's Italian-American culture of crime and violence. Scorsese wrote and directed the film based on his own experience of growing up there. The role De Niro played brought him closer to his own Italian heritage. "In the end, my roots are in Italy," says De Niro. "I am honored to have become an Italian citizen." (Italy officially granted him citizenship in October 2006.)

The Houses of SoHo
Brick facades and cast iron fire escape ladders are characteristic here. De Niro has a very strong tie with this quarter, where the former studio of his artist father is located.

"New York represents, first of all, my home. There are times when I find I am willing to stay at home, feeling the need to spend time with my family. And, there are times, when, as one of the most beautiful cities in the world, New York beckons to me to explore. There is no other place where you feel this same energy, this pulse of life."

"We shot the film for three weeks in Los Angeles and two in New York," De Niro recounts. "As an East Coast actor, it was one of my first West Coast experiences. In *Mean Streets*, I realized how connected I am to New York, my city of origin. I'm a New Yorker. This is my home. There is a physical difference, a sense of belonging that binds me here instinctively."

In Francis Ford Coppola's *The Godfather Part II* (1974), playing one of his most iconic characters, Don Vito Corleone, De Niro explores the complex mechanisms of a New York mafia family. As Travis Bickle in *Taxi Driver* (1976), De Niro reveals, with equal fascination, the underworld of New York taxi drivers, when he plays an ex-Vietnam marine who suffers from chronic insomnia. All night, his character drives through the jungle of neighborhoods, encountering prostitution, pornography, and the dark sides of the great Metropolis, with all its contradictions and hypocrisy.

In *New York, New York* (1977), directed by Scorsese, De Niro's character, Jimmy Doyle, paints an indelible portrait of the city's vivid music and jazz scene. An egotistical saxophonist, Jimmy brings an ironic twist to New York's rhythm and song, while Liza Minnelli plays an ambassador to the City, singing the song he wrote for her, "New York, New York."

Little Italy
Detail of the Little Italy neighborhood, home of the famous Ferrara Bakery and Cafe. Founded in 1892 on Grand Street, the bakery is a classic example of a business handed down for generations.

Mulberry Street
This is one of the best-known streets in Little Italy, the neighborhood where Robert De Niro grew up with his mother and which was the setting for *Mean Streets*, the first movie he acted in under Martin Scorsese's direction.

"I'm a New Yorker. This is my home.
There is a physical difference, a sense of belonging
that binds me here instinctively."

In another Scorsese film, *Raging Bull* (1980), De Niro portrays his Oscar winning role of Jake LaMotta, a working class boxer from the Bronx striving to lift himself out of the ghetto and into the American Dream.

"I am linked to every role I play in some way. One of my strongest connections is with the movie *Once Upon a Time in America* (1984) by Sergio Leone, and the character David Aaronson, (a.k.a. Noodles)," De Niro confides. The movie chronicles the vicissitudes of Noodles and his friends as they make the transition from childhood to adolescence and adulthood, while developing as businessmen in the world of crime. In the film, their shift from the Jewish ghetto to the criminal underworld is paralleled by the era as New York shifts from Prohibition to post-Prohibition.

In *Goodfellas* (1990), De Niro explores the story behind another one of New York's iconic boroughs, Brooklyn, through a powerful crime scene set in Brownsville.

De Niro is a true New York "insider". Born in Greenwich Village on August 17, 1943, he grew up in an artistic environment created by his father, the abstract expressionist painter and sculptor Robert De Niro Sr., and his mother, Virginia Admiral, painter and poet. "My father was half Italian and half Irish. My paternal great-grandparents were from Ferrazzano, in the province of Campobasso, when they immigrated in 1890. My mother's background was English, German, French, and Dutch," he recounts.

Street Art
There are still graffiti on the walls of various quarters of the Downtown area. Here is an example on the facade of a building on East 9th Street, in East Village.

Downtown: a taxi whizzes by one of the many manholes that emit sewer gas.

De Niro feels most strongly that he is Italian-American. After his parents divorced, he grew up with his mother in Little Italy. His father, who died of cancer in 1993, had a studio-loft in SoHo during the Bohemian 1950s. The still intact studio is a slice of the long-gone New York artists' scene. Its walls are covered in fabric and carpet and adorned with African masks, vibrant paintings, and drawings. It is a corner of the past, of precious memories that De Niro Jr. has helped to keep alive.

De Niro grew up alongside such great artistic figures as Jackson Pollock, Anaïs Nin, Willem de Kooning, Henry Miller and Tennessee Williams. His father was one of the prominent figurative expressionists of the New York art scene in 1946 when, at the age of only 24, he had his first solo show at the Art of This Century Gallery of Peggy Guggenheim on 57th Street. Even the famed critic Clement Greenberg, who discovered Jackson Pollock, wrote about De Niro Sr.'s artwork in *The Nation*. Many of the paintings are now at The Museum of Modern Art (MoMA), The Metropolitan Museum of Art, and the Whitney Museum of American Art. Today, some of his father's paintings hang from the walls of his Tribeca Grill restaurant and The Greenwich Hotel.

DUMBO

New York is also its streets, so rich in life and surprises, such as these railway tracks, which are a vestige of the former industrial zone in Brooklyn known as Down Under the Manhattan Bridge Overpass.

> "New York is contagious.
> More and more I feel here that
> I don't want to miss a single moment."

Tribeca
Triangle Below Canal Street is the neighborhood that Robert De Niro has helped to revive, partly due to the Tribeca Film Festival, founded in 2002.

A Mermaid
Originally intended as decoration for the fountain in Place de la Concorde in Paris, this statue stands in front of an elegant building in the Tribeca neighborhood.

The SoHo neighborhood that now surrounds his father's loft has been transformed into elegant boutiques and galleries. Today's SoHo is a hub for shopping, chic restaurants, and curious tourists who walk up and down streets with buildings in the neighborhood's typical cast iron architecture. "I want to keep my father's studio alive to show to my children and grandchildren," says De Niro. "Sometimes I still come here to sit and reflect."

The art studio has become a kind of "shrine to memory" and a source of inspiration for De Niro. He dedicated the first feature film he produced, *Bronx* (1993), to his father. In the film, he is a young Italian boy, the son of a bus driver who spends his days imitating the Bronx boss Sonny and ends up with his own troubled lot, and a life of crime.

Another place that inspires De Niro is Washington Square Park in Greenwich Village where he used to go with his father as a child. Today, it's a park where many artists and musicians go to play music, and where many New Yorkers like to play chess.

De Niro is more than just an acting talent. As a director, he shot the stunning *The Good Shepherd* (2006), based on the early history of the CIA, as told through the semi-fictional story of one man's life. "Working as a director is very different to being an actor," he explains.

"You must invest much more of your time, and think every detail through to the end. It's a different energy, more like being the captain of a ship."

"Tribeca is a world in itself, like a village in a city with large tree-lined avenues and parks set along rows of luxury condominiums, small shops, boutiques, art galleries and historic buildings," says De Niro. "You can see the Powell Building on Hudson Street, built in 1892 by Carrère and Hastings, the Art Deco New York Telephone Company Building at 140 West Street, the New York Mercantile Exchange at 6 Harrison Street, and the beautiful white Neo-Renaissance buildings dating from 1865 at 73 Worth Street."

Tribeca (Triangle Below Canal Street) is a small neighborhood, consisting of a series of roadways and tiny streets that gather around and crisscross a signature triangle intersection.

It's one of the most trendy, fashionable, and expensive neighborhoods in Manhattan, where many New Yorkers dream of living. Robert De Niro believed in Tribeca when nobody else did, and invested in what was then almost a wasteland. Now, urban legend says, he owns most of the buildings.

Reflections
The heart of the financial district near the Tribeca neighborhood is distinguished by its many glass skyscrapers.

The **Tribeca Film Festival**.

De Niro started the revival of the area in 1993 in collaboration with producer Jane Rosenthal. After 9/11, they created the television drama series TriBeCa to support the neighborhood's rebirth. From the series, the Tribeca Film Festival was born in 2002, going on to become one of the most important film events in the world. "With Jane," says De Niro, "we wanted to contribute to the revitalization of Downtown around the Twin Towers that had been destroyed. Each year, on the last day of the Festival, we have the Tribeca fair which has become a veritable tradition," he shares. "We are very proud of it because it's a celebration of our sense of community."

Now, the new World Trade Center area is growing, with a breathable sense of "la dolce vita". Quite near the Hudson River, with its parks and restaurants, you can sit along a harbor laced with yachts and sailboats and look at the palm trees of the World Financial Center's Winter Garden.

During the Tribeca Film Festival, in April, the neighborhood is teeming with life, events and celebrities, while the rest of the year it hums as a hub for creative minds from fashion, film, and the culinary arts. It is now also home to some of the City's most notable restaurants.

"We never imagined that the Festival would become so large," reflects De Niro, "and that every year we would have so many volunteers from all over the world here to help us."

Robert De Niro has excelled in another great art form – hospitality. He not only created the renowned Tribeca Grill, but The Greenwich Hotel and its restaurant, Locanda Verde. His downtown production headquarters includes private screening rooms and promotion and production offices in the Tribeca Film Center on Greenwich Street in the old Martinson Coffee Building. The building also houses the famous Tribeca Grill, co-property of the actor, who has brought the flavors of a modern Mediterranean American cuisine to the neighborhood.

The Seventh Art
Robert De Niro at the premiere of a film during the 2014 Tribeca Film Festival, the major cinema event co-founded by the actor and Jane Rosenthal.

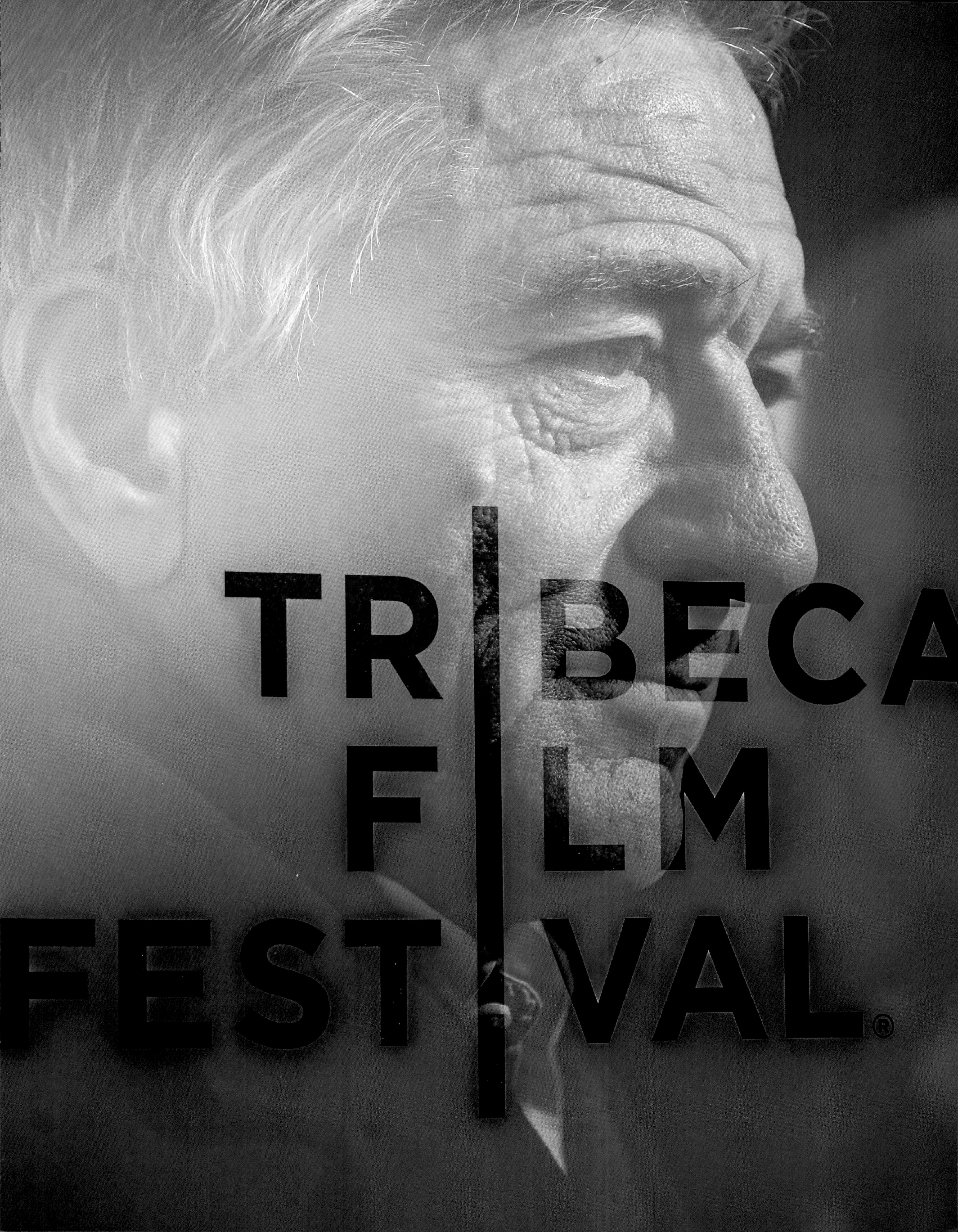
TRIBECA
FILM
FESTIVAL®

"New York teaches us that we must take chances in life, and that we must make the right decisions. It teaches us to have confidence and believe in our dreams, to never give up."

De Niro is also co-founder of Nobu Restaurants, for which he helps provide creative direction. "I love sashimi," he says. "Nobu is a true creative, an artist of the food genre." Nobu New York is a gastronomic temple that adds a mythical touch of Japan to New York.

The Greenwich Hotel is another De Niro creation, in collaboration with renowned architect and designer David Rockwell. "I wanted a space that I would like to live in, with a warm atmosphere," says De Niro. "Many of the hotels where I stay around the world are wonderful, but very cold. We also wanted to create something that fits in seamlessly with the spirit of the neighborhood."

The most spectacular feature of The Greenwich Hotel is the rooftop penthouse, with a terrace, garden and the stunning Shibui Spa that conceals a pool lit by lanterns and nestled under the bamboo roof of a 250-year old Japanese country house. The house was transported here from Kyoto and reconstructed by thirteen Japanese craftsmen.

The Greenwich Hotel
The boutique hotel co-founded in 2008 by Robert De Niro looks more like a private home, and boasts a unique and elegant style. Here we see the side with small balconies overlooking the garden.

The Penthouse
A sitting room in the rooftop penthouse of the Greenwich Hotel. It was created by designer Axel Vervoordt and architect Tatsuro Miki and is distinguished by its taste and the attention paid to the materials used.

The **Locanda Verde**, one of the restaurants De Niro has launched.

The hotel's restaurant, Locanda Verde, was created, in collaboration with the famous chef Andrew Carmellini, as a variation of an Italian tavern, accented with Italian-style furniture and shelves filled with wines and books. Among its specialties is the renowned "porchetta of the house." Karen DeMasco, a master of custard desserts, famously indulges her guests in regional "fantasies" such as Neapolitan spumoni with cherries.

"We took a lot of time to think through the concept of what Locanda Verde would be," explains De Niro. "I find that with Italian restaurants it is difficult to find the right idea, because there are so many of them. When you are designing a restaurant, you are always looking to create something a little different. Celebrity is not enough," he adds. "The food must stand on its own. One restaurant I always liked is Tavern on the Green. I remember as a child I was able to see films played there. It was a magical place for me."

"I don't really feel like a Hollywood icon. It's not like I wake up in the morning fighting a slap on the shoulder to congratulate myself!" De Niro laughs. "I am first of all a New Yorker. I try

The **Tavern on The Green** restaurant in Central Park.

to lead a respectful life as a member of the City, like everyone else."

As the father of a family living in New York, De Niro has a deep sense of community that binds him to the City, to the tragedies that struck, like 9/11, the financial crisis, and to its future. "I have children and grandchildren, and as a father you are always thinking about their future," he shares. "You hope everything will go well for them and that they will always be healthy. My life here has been good," he says. "In the same way, I've always recovered from challenges; I know that New York is a wonderful city that will recov-er too. I've always felt that New York will never give up."

What does Robert De Niro wish for his children and future generations of New Yorkers? "To have the courage to take risks. If you do not take a risk, you'll never find out what's possible," he says. "New York teaches us that we must take chances in life, and that we must make the right decisions. It teaches us to have confidence and believe in our dreams, to never give up," De Niro proposes. "Perhaps New York, with its races, cultures, and people who come from everywhere to chase their dreams, is a mirror of existence itself."

JAMES FRANCO

The "Artist" of the City

For him, New York is another way of experimenting, of producing art. James Franco is a real artist. He is an actor. He is a filmmaker. He is a writer. He is a teacher. He is a poet. He is a painter. He is a producer. His polyhedric soul finds its quest in the thousands possibilities of creativity that New York offers. "New York has everything I love. LA does too, but you have to look harder in LA. In New York something is happening on every block, every minute," he explains.

Born in Palo Alto, California, Franco is the eldest of three brothers (one of them, Dave, is also an actor). His mother is a poetess and a writer from Russian descent with a Jewish background, while his father, of Portuguese and Swedish descent, was in a Silicon Valley business. He briefly studied English and Drama at the University of California before pursuing a career as an actor, getting a role in the television series *Freaks and Geeks*. Since then he has developed his career more and more, while never forgetting his nature as an artist and being active in every field in which his talent could develop. In the meantime he won a Golden Globe Award in 2001's TV biographical film *James Dean*, with a stunning performance of the iconic star, he played in independent movies like *Sonny* (2002) by Nicholas Cage, and he took

> New York has everything I love. In New York something is happening on every block, every minute.

a role, among the many movies he did, in the series *Spider-Man* (2002), in *Tristan & Isolde* (2006), in *Pineapple Express* (2008), in *Milk* (2008) alongside acclaimed actor Sean Penn playing Harvey Milk, in *Howl* (2010) as legendary Beat poet Allen Ginsberg, and in *127 Hours* (2010), the true story of a climber's tragic accident in Utah, in *Rise of the Planet of the Apes* (2011), and the Harmony Korine-directed crime drama *Spring Breakers* (2013)," as a magician in *Oz the Great and Powerful* (2013) and *Palo Alto* (2013).

Franco decided also to go on studying, at UCLA, as a creative writing major in 2008, as well as in New York. And it was during this time, while working here as an actor, that his relationship with the City developed, living in it like a real New Yorker and discovering it day by day. "At the end of August, 2008, I came to live in New York for the first time. I found my first apartment in the West Village, as it was close to NYU, where I was enrolled in film school at Tisch," he remembers. Then he was even taking courses in fiction writing at Brooklyn College and studying poetry at Warren Wilson College in North Carolina. In 2010, he was even accepted at Yale University, pursuing a Ph.D. in English, while he had earned his M.F.A. from Columbia.

"And I love taking the subway in New York.
It's great to watch people,
it's like being in an underground world."

A panoramic view of Midtown in early evening from the observation deck of the Empire State Building.

Light installations at the Bleecker Street/Broadway Lafayette Street subway station.

The former Manhattan Main Line subway station at City Hall.

In 2011, he finished his master's degree in filmmaking at NYU and was accepted into the Rhode Island School of Design's literature and creative writing program. His colleagues said that, to keep track with his studying, he was even reading books and studying during breaks on the set.

Since he was a child he has always loved reading. And, besides being an actor, James Franco is a filmmaker, getting inspiration from literature. He directed the film versions of William Faulkner's *As I Lay Dying* (2013) and of Cormac McCarthy's 1973 novella *Child of God* (2013) with Scott Haze. Fashion, another of his great passions, convinced him to produce the documentary *The Director*, direct-

ed by Christina Voros, a look at the life and work of former Gucci fashion designer Frida Giannini.

He got used to some typical New York habits. Like walking... "When I am in LA I drive a lot, but here in New York I go on long walks and listen to audio books or music," he explains about his living in the City. And then he got used to another habit, beating the traffic... "I started taking the subway to go to Columbia University, where I did a creative writing program. I also went to Columbia's library all the time, to study and to read books in the quiet room section. I really like the Columbia campus," he says. "And I love taking the subway in New York. It's great to watch people, it's like being in an underground world."

A **Broadway** street sign.
Skyscrapers at **Times Square**.

Franco has been painting since he was in his high school years and he attended the California State Summer School of the Arts and he has done many exhibitions, while his paintings are featured in his book *Hollywood Dreaming* (Insight Editions, 2014) together with his poems. But New York inspired him in this direction too, as he is part of the local art scene. "In 2010, I presented my first solo exhibition, *The Dangerous Book Four Boys*, at The Clocktower Gallery in New York City. Curated by Alanna Heiss, the show featured videos, drawings, sculptures and installations based on childhood experiences. The space was at the top of an operating court building, so you had to go through a metal detector to get to the gallery. The space had a great history, Basquiat and Gordon Matta Clark both showed there," he says.

Another great love of James Franco's relationship with New York is theater. "I love theater. When I was a teenager, I used to go from Palo Alto, where I was born and I lived, to San Francisco to see plays. When I am in New York, and I have any free time, I spend it going to see plays on and off Broadway," he confesses. Franco made his Broadway stage debut in the role of George in a revival of John Steinbeck's *Of Mice and Men* by Anna D. Shapiro. "I have always been a big Broadway fan, you can just check all the tickets I have from the last 15 years. So the missing piece for me was just to be part of it and I was looking for the perfect piece to do. *Of Mice and Men* is a universal story, which will always be topical."

Franco volunteered for The Art of Elysium charity, which helps children with serious medical

Illuminated signs at Times Square.

"I love theater... When I am in New York, and I have any free time, I spend it going to see plays on and off Broadway."

conditions, and taught a class, at New York University, in feature filmmaking and production, besides having always been available to support the work of his students and read screenplays, which he might produce too. He loves to be part of the New York community and a mentor for upcoming artists.

"I love schools, learning and teaching and being around people who have the same interests as I do. At the same time, I like to support the work of young talent. My students are very important to me," he points out.

"When I collaborate I like it to be an open and safe relationship. With Gia Coppola, whom I chose to adapt and direct my short stories book *Palo Alto* into a movie, I gave her tons of freedom. My single, biggest creative decision is to choose the artist.

"After that, I really want him or her to bring his or her own vision. I am not going to control it." And in this, he also represents the great spirit and freedom of a polyhedric and metropolitan City like New York, where every creative and talented mind can find its own voice.

Lights in Times Square
Digital screens and billboards in Times Square are some of the most iconic advertising spaces for the famous Broadway shows.

JACK HUSTON

An Englishman in the City

His talent is so various, all-encompassing, and vibrant that he is one of the most diversified actors of his generation, capable of investing even small roles with a great degree of attention and sensitivity.

"New York, for me, is the center of inspiration, of ideas and possibilities, with that incredible energy that no other metropolis has," he says.

His relationship with the City started when he was a child, dreaming about it, watching beautiful films and seeing locations and moments of street life, like romances and adventures.

Jack Huston, born in 1982, is English, but he also became a New Yorker too, while he was living here during the shooting of the TV serial *Boardwalk Empire.*

> New York, for me, is the center of inspiration, of ideas and possibilities, with that incredible energy that no other metropolis has.

"But I am always here, in and out, as I keep on working in the City, and I simply love it here. Here I have been falling in love as well, with my girlfriend Shannan Click and also my daughter, Sage, was born here in 2013. So I have, for sure, a special connection now with New York," he says. "The good thing about New York is that after a while, when you live here, you really feel a New Yorker. It is different than when you visit it as a tourist or when you are here for a short time. When you really live here, New York gets into you," he says.

An actor, but also a producer, for the movie inspired by the script *Hunting & Gathering*, directed by his brother Matthew Huston and written by Matthew together with the artist Melanie Gilligan, Jack has a special sensibility for looking at things that only an artist has. He also likes writing and painting. "When I first arrived in New York I was amazed by the energy of the City. Many people say it, but for me it was something even more special and different. And particularly unique for a city," he says. "When I was twenty-one years old, I went from London to Los Angeles and only after that did I come to New York.

"It was really very different here for me, but I was fascinated by the City, as, for me, it has the best of LA and the best of London. New York has a sense in everything, at the same time there is always a rush to go somewhere, as there is always something happening somewhere," he explains. "What it is that is different in New York is that the people are all in the street and life is all around you."

Jack is the grandchild of the great filmmaker John Huston, son of the American actor Tony Huston and the painter and noblewoman Lady Margot Lavinia Cholmondeley, with paternal aunt Anjelica Huston and paternal half uncle Danny, amazing actors and stars. Jack has the art of acting in his blood, and in

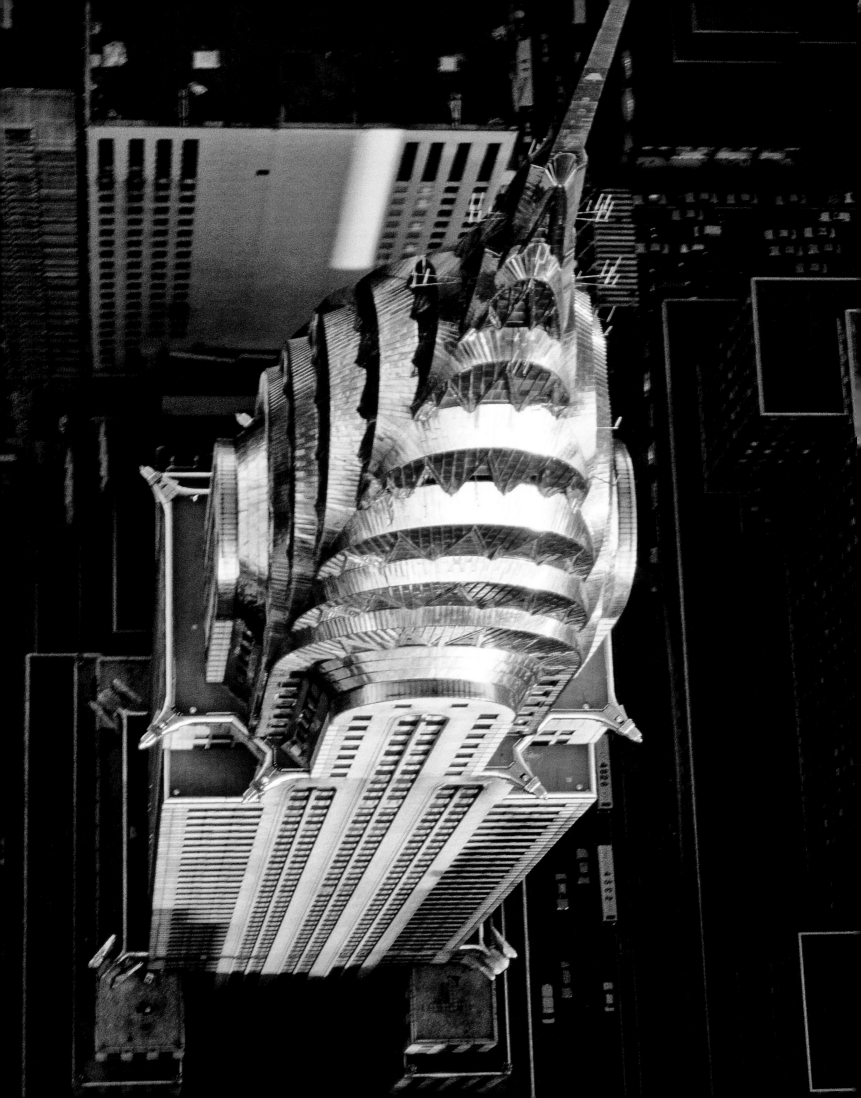

"... the Chrysler Building... every time I see it I think that the romance in New York will never end."

his soul. Acting for him was a passion and love at first sight.

Jack has always wanted to be an actor and he decided to pursue this profession when he was six years old, after playing in the title role in a school production of *Peter Pan*. He attended the dramatic institute Hurtwood House and he started his career with different roles in many films, among them the American poet Gerard Malanga in *Factory Girl*, an aspiring rock star in *Not Fade Away*, directed by David Chase, the creator of *The Sopranos*, *The Twilight Saga: Eclipse*, *Wilde Salome* directed by Al Pacino, *Night Train to Lisbon*, and *American Hustle* by David O. Russell.

But it was in New York that Jack developed one of his most famous roles, as Richard Harrow, a severely disfigured World War I marksman turned gangster, in the TV serial *Boardwalk Empire*, which narrates the story of the gangster world of the past in Atlantic City.

"For this serial we have been playing a bit everywhere, in and around New York, not so much in Atlantic City, where boardwalks and casinos are still interesting places, but mostly in some studios in Brooklyn, by the river. But the good thing is that I had the possibility to get to know the City really very well during that time."

Also, in New York he played another big role in his career in *Kill Your Darlings* by John Krokidas,

in which he is a young Jack Kerouac, involved in a mysterious murder at Columbia University. In this film, you can also discover the atmosphere of Columbia University and its beautiful campus, which you can still visit today. It was founded in 1754 as King's College by a royal charter of King George II of England and is the oldest institution of higher learning in the state of New York and the fifth oldest in the United States. It was moved, in 1897, to its present location, on Morningside Heights at 116th Street and Broadway. The new campus was created like an Athenian agora, and comprises the largest single collection of McKim, Mead & White buildings in existence.

The beautiful Low Memorial Library, in Roman classical style, dominates the plaza, with its green fields, while the College Walk goes through all the main buildings, such as the Butler Library, Pupin Hall, and St. Paul's Chapel. "Being Kerouac in this movie has been a wonderful experience, as we have been discovering the New York of that time as well as the academic world. There are also funny stories with us in the library. The story is about the real murder of David Kammerer by Lucien Carr, who is played by Dane DeHaan. Some other Beat Generation artists were involved, besides Kerouac – Allen Ginsberg, played by Daniel Radcliffe, and William Burroughs, played by Ben Foster," he explains.

An aerial view of the **Chrysler Building**.

An **East Village** restaurant.

"The movie was taking place at Columbia University and it has been so amazing to be part of it, because I discovered New York through their eyes and words. They lived in the moment, like I have the feeling a lot of artists still do in New York. At that point Jack Kerouac was not the writer we know, but just a young guy trying to find his voice. It was a film played in the past, but it reminds me of the New York of today, where a lot of artists still come, full of dreams and trying to make it."

Jack, as an artist himself, realized how it was living in the City. "When I used to visit New York I enjoyed it, but I was not a New Yorker, I just found a lot of fun here, of course, but I was missing a lot of things," he thinks. "I was just stopping by, visiting friends, but I was not delving deeply into the soul of the City. But if you do live here, it is another experience – you find your local neighborhood, you play pool in a bar or you go to have a beer in a pub or you go for a coffee in one of the many lovely coffee shops. You find out that New York is a place to discover day by day, in moments of everyday life."

New Yorkers love their neighborhood, which becomes, at some point, like their own "village" in the big City. So everybody here is looking for their own neighborhood at some point, the one they feel they belong to or feel closer to their sensibility.

A shop in **Greenwich Village**.

"I lived in Soho for a while, then, with my girl-friend, we moved to the East Village that since then has been home for me. I love its bars and restaurants. I have my favorite Japanese place there to go to eat sushi. The coffee shops are numerous on the streets," he says. "One of my favorite places is Tompkins Square Park, which also has a wonderful dog run. It used to be dangerous, but now it is really a lovely place. Nearly all the actors in *Boardwalk Empire* lived in this area, only a few blocks from each other. I always like taking my dogs there."

Music is another universe that fascinates Jack, and in New York he can find a lot of different genres.

"I like going to listen to live music, but there is a place, owned by a friend of mine, that I like mostly. It is called *Electric Room*, in Chelsea, and I like the sessions they do there. In LA I co-own *The Writer's Room*. I kind of prefer places that have a special flair and their own personality," he says.

Jack also enjoys the possibilities you can find outside the City, as well as in it. "New York is also a place where you can easily reach the woods and the beach. And I love all the beautiful nature you can find outside of the City. I like the possibilities to drive outside it instead of being only inside it," he points out, confessing he also likes the Hamptons.

"I like renting a place at East Hampton for the summer, as the beach, the sea and nature are really beautiful there. New York is a season city, so it is amazing in spring, when all the trees are in flower, in the autumn with the foliage, the changing of the leaves with their marvelous colors, but it is very cold in winter and terribly hot and humid in the summer. So a lot of New Yorkers get another place in the Hamptons during the summer. Another place that I really like is the town of Woodstock, in the Catskill Hills, where the famous rock festival took place. I love going out there a lot as well," he continues.

He remembers then that, in New York, he has memories thanks to his family. "I, my brother Matthew and my sister Laura are all very close to my aunt Anjelica, and we have been with her, several times, on set in some of her movies. I remember especially when she played in *The Royal Tenenbaums* in New York. My sister lived with her during that time, and I came to visit as well," he remembers.

Neighborhood Life

A pianist performing in Washington Square Park, which offers many an occasion for relaxing outdoors and listening to good music.

The Villages

A popular restaurant in West Village that features Mediterranean cuisine. New Yorkers are proud of their neighborhoods and enjoy them to the full.

"What it is that is different in New York is that the people
are all in the street and life is all around you."

A **mural** on East 2nd Street, in East Village.
Famous musicians are portrayed on this Greenwich Village mural.

The family home, "111 Archer Avenue", can be found in Harlem, at 339 Covent Avenue and 144th Street, while the hotel from which Gene Hackman is evicted is The Waldorf Astoria, at 301 Park Avenue, in Midtown. Among the other film locations there is also the National Museum of the American Indian, on Bowling Green, in Lower Manhattan. "It is incredible how many places you can really discover in Manhattan, but also in its districts. It is really a place where you can always find something new."

Another thing Jack gets fascinated by are the colors of New York. "When I think of a color for the City I have silver in mind. New York glitters like it. It is very difficult to choose a specific color, the right color, as you see so many here every day. But I know it is something metal and gleaming white," he reflects. "It is the color that you also find in many skyscrapers, another element of Manhattan which has always fascinated me. My favorite one is the Chrysler Building, as I remember it from when I saw it the first time in the movies I used to watch in my infancy. It was then that I fell in love with New York for the first time to find out that, in reality, New York is even more beautiful. I have some friends with an apartment in Madison Square Park, with a terrace overlooking the Chrysler Building, and every time I see it I think that the romance in New York will never end."

SIRI HUSTVEDT

The "Psyche" of the City

Her blue eyes are deep as an iced lake, and look like they could read your soul. The American novelist and essayist Siri Hustvedt is one of the most renowned contemporary writers of the New York scene. Her novels and essays are profound and filled with her well-known and intensely dramatic note of sensuality.

Like her writing, her townhouse home in Brooklyn's Park Slope is an intimate and introspective reflection of her spirit. Each floor is a place to browse through like chapters in a novel, discovering amazing glimpses of life. With its beauty and originality, the home reflects the chameleon-like diversity of New York.

A similar intensity in the words on Hustvedt's pages leads you into the soul of the modern metropolis. "Writing is a need, a calling, an imperative in my life. It has nothing to do with 'liking.' I am compelled to do it and have felt this way since I was very young. When I write I feel more alive."

"New York inspires me because it has tremendous variety. Park Slope in Brooklyn is one piece in a larger puzzle of the many villages that make up the city, but it is familiar and intimate to me," she explains.

Her New York is psychological, introspective and deeply penetrating, as in the novels *What I Loved*, *The Sorrows of America*, and *The Summer Without Men*.

"What fascinates me about the city are the relationships between people, their connections to one another, how their lives cross, meet, mingle and disappear in a multitude of worlds," she says.

Born in Northfield, Minnesota in 1955, Hustvedt moved to New York to attend Columbia University. In New York, she met the love of her life – her soul mate, and now husband, best-selling author Paul Auster. Their daughter, the singer and actress Sophie Auster, was born in 1987.

While Sophie lives in trendy, mythical Tribeca, Siri explains that her New York is Brooklyn, and specifically, Park Slope. It is a place that, she believes, truly reflects her sensibilities. "For me, New York is, first of all, Park Slope. It is a comfortable neighborhood of late nineteenth century houses and apartment buildings, with the marvelous Prospect Park, the largest park in the city after Central Park. It's filled with pedestrians and cyclists, soccer, cricket and softball players, people on picnics, and even wildlife. I like walking down Seventh Avenue listening to snippets of conversation in many languages. I like watching the children. There are many in our neighborhood. I frequent the same stores and know the shopkeepers and grocers. Park Slope often has the feel of a village, but with less gossip," Hustvedt says.

> For me, New York is also home. It is a city big enough to remain mysterious in parts, and it is constantly changing.

The everyday **atmosphere in Park Slope** is similar to that of a small town.

Hustvedt prefers Brooklyn to Manhattan for its discreet, homey feel. "Home is familiarity and repetition. It provides me with the safety of sameness. We all internalize the architecture of home, not just consciously but unconsciously as well. I don't need to look for a light switch. My arm reaches for it before I have thought about it. The lack of strain is why people feel comfortable at home and why moving can be stressful," she believes. "For me, New York is also home. It is a city big enough to remain mysterious in parts, and it is constantly changing. No one can know the whole city and that may be why it remains surprising and unpredictable."

She talks about her house, which, like everything in New York, contains a story. "I looked at houses in Park Slope for about a year before I found the house where we now live. It's a four-story row house built in 1892 and had most of its original detail intact. My husband Paul and I were both taken with it. People think of New York as a city of skyscrapers but it is also a city of brownstones and townhouses, and these structures are part of an older New York, part of the city's memory."

Her New York is also a place of the things that have meaning beyond the superficial glamour which first strikes the eyes of the occasional visitor.

A street in **Park Slope** lined with trees and brownstone houses.

"We have lived in the house for almost 19 years now, and my favorite room is the library. It's filled with mine and my husband's books. My favorite piece of furniture is the red table that my architect sister, Ingrid Hustvedt, designed for our dining room. Many people we love have sat around that table."

"Paul and I mostly like to stay home, or, occasionally, go out for dinner in some local restaurant such as Rose Water or Al Di Là. It's in the familiarity of the everyday things that I discover the soul of New York, the one which is closest to us."

Hustvedt is interested in the psychological and biological aspects of human experience, including the writing of novels and a central question: where do works of fiction come from? "I once gave a lecture in London entitled, 'Why One Story and Not Another?' A fiction writer can theoretically write anything, but that's not how it works. The writer is guided by a sense of right and wrong, which obviously has nothing to do with the literal truth of the text. I am deeply interested in this question. To cut a long story short, the answer is at once sociological, psychological, and neurobiological."

"I like the diversity of the people who live in New York, and I like the many languages that are spoken here. Living here, one encounters not just one, but many worlds.

View of **Prospect Park** in autumn.

"New York inspires me because it has tremendous variety."

"Charles Dickens once said of his city: 'If you don't like London, you don't like life.' If this were true for London, then it can only be truer about New York. The mixture of cultures makes this place particularly interesting and exciting. And, despite a few minor exceptions, New York is, generally, very tolerant," she says.

"New York has many subcultures. I described the art world in my novel *What I Loved*. Because I am fascinated by psychoanalysis, psychiatry and neuroscience, I have attended conferences and lectured on these subjects in the city. I was also a volunteer who taught writing to psychiatric in-patients at New York Hospital. The narrator of my novel *The Sorrows of an American* is a psychiatrist. My research in these fields and my experience in the hospital helped me to write the book. Every writer is a voyeur, after all, a person who watches and observes others. In New York, there is lots of material for literature."

A Boat Ride

An electric boat on the lake in Prospect Park, which is filled with algae. These rides start off from the historic Boathouse founded in 1905.

"Park Slope in Brooklyn is one piece in a larger puzzle of the many villages that make up the city, but it is familiar and intimate to me."

The **Prospect Park lake** in winter.

Her favorite places in Manhattan are very intimate, too. "I love the Frick Collection, between 70th Street and 5th Avenue. It's enclosed in a beautiful residence with a garden. It is a small collection of major works, including Vermeer, Goya, Chardin and others. Unlike the immense museums in New York, it's cozy and never very crowded."

New York continues to be a special place for Siri Hustvedt. "I feel I have roots in this city, and my habits and familiarity with it are certainly part of the connection. At the same time, the city's ability to adapt to changing circumstances has made me think of it as a character, a changing, developing being. Despite my attachment to the city, I also think I am a person who could probably live in various places. Take me anywhere, and I would no doubt discover the pleasures and idiosyncrasies of another geographical location. Still, I grew up in a small town, and I do not want to return to provincial life. I like feeling that I am part of something much larger than me, that I am one person among millions in a great metropolis."

SPIKE LEE
The "Soul" of the City

The power of humanity: proud and strong, able to sparkle, to feel and find reason even in the darkest moments. In the background, jazzy blues plays with suffering intensity, following the destiny of the characters.

Spike Lee is one of today's most influential movie directors. He is also an actor, producer and writer. As a professor at New York University (NYU), Lee remains in touch with students and young people, and ordinary daily life.

The works of Spike Lee depict New York's Afro-American identity and its struggle for the recognition of equal rights. He shows us boldness and determination, a sense of community, engagement and activism. In movies like *Jungle Fever* and *Malcolm X*, he explores contemporary life through the black community, family, relationships, race relations, urban crime and poverty, and political issues. Lee's inspiration comes from idols like Malcolm X and Martin Luther King, who have influenced his body of work. "I have never thought to represent the whole Afro-American community; I have only spread out my ideas. Some New Yorkers think like me and some don't," he says.

New York for him can be heard beneath notes of jazz and blues music that express the intense feelings of its subjects who inhabit the City. "New York is in me," says Spike Lee. "It's part of my blood and my soul, and in my movies I've tried to represent its different aspects. New York is not one, but an infinite number of worlds combined. I love New York, its people and its energy, which doesn't exist in any other place in the world. What makes New York are its people and their great energy."

"This is the greatest city in the world, but that won't last long if there are only rich people living here," Lee says. "People need to feel they can afford to live in the City, to give their children an adequate education and send them to good public schools. Unfortunately, if we go on like this, a lot of people won't be able to afford to be here any more."

Lee's New York is the one found in everyday life. And not just Manhattan, but also Brooklyn, the borough where you can forget the bright lights of the City and dig deeper into the nuances of the American soul. In his films, he reveals his special relationship with Brooklyn. "I have done different chronicles of Brooklyn in *She's Gotta Have It*, *Do the Right Thing*, *He Got Game*, *Clockers*, and *Crooklyn*, which is one of the most autobiographical movies I've made. I have been showing parts of the City that tourists don't usually see. And also its forgotten elements," he explains when we meet in his NYU studio.

> I love New York, its people and its energy, which doesn't exist in any other place in the world. What makes New York are its people and their great energy.

> ## "New York is first of all the story you hide inside yourself."

Spike Lee's New York is also the university world, which, he believes, keeps him close to "real" people. "I love teaching as much as I like making movies. I've been teaching different courses in film at NYU for many years. New York is also the City of students, of the youth who come here full of ideas and dreams, and who believe in the possibilities that they can find here."

In the film *Red Hook Summer*, in a kind of Brooklyn genesis, Lee tells the story of a 13-year old boy from Atlanta sent to live with his preacher grandfather in Red Hook, an emerging neighborhood in Brooklyn that still retains its local character. The story reveals facets of the filmmaker himself, as much as of all the youth growing up in a place as diverse and metropolitan as New York.

"New York is first of all the story you hide inside yourself. I grew up in Cobble Hill and lived for many years in Fort Greene," he says. Fort Greene today is considered a sort of "new Harlem," and is the home of the Brooklyn Academy of Music (BAM). Spike Lee moved to the Upper East Side, but still feels a strong connection with the place. "Fort Greene is still my favorite neighborhood, even if it's now gentrified. Fort Greene Park was near my house, between Washington Street and Vanderbilt Avenue, and I love walking by the coffee shops and African restaurants of DeKalb Avenue. In the end, New York is also the place of memories and roots."

Spike Lee was born in 1957 in Atlanta. His mother was a teacher of arts and Afro-American literature and his father, William James Edward Lee III, was a jazz musician and composer. He had three younger siblings, who have all collaborated in the making of his films. His family moved to Brooklyn when he was a child and he enrolled in Morehouse College, a historically Afro-American college. Later, Lee completed a Master of Fine Arts in Film & Television at New York's Tisch School of the Arts.

"It was in college that I became really passionate about cinema," says Lee. "I was at the Clark College, which is now called Clark Atlanta University, and I had a great professor, Dr Herb Eichelberger. It's thanks to him that I became one of America's first Afro-American directors," Lee recounts. "At that time when I told the friends I grew up with in New York that I wanted to be a filmmaker, they looked at me with irony. They didn't believe me."

Brooklyn Bridge
After a heavy snowfall the bridge is used by very few persons, a detail that makes this scene special and romantic.

The townhouses with front stairs are typical of **Brooklyn Heights**.

> "New York is not one,
> but an infinite number
> of worlds combined."

"Above all, I must thank my mother for her passion for the arts," Lee says. "She took me, as a child, to watch movies, to the theater, and to Broadway musicals. At the beginning, I didn't really want to go, but once I saw the show, I was always very happy. My father was a musician and from him I took the love for music."

New York, for Spike Lee, is also the world of music and musicals. "I have always been fascinated by Broadway and by its musicals, like by all the jazz, blues and music night clubs. New York is the City of great music and sounds, and it expresses its beat with the stories it tells, and through the people who made it."

After achieving huge success, Spike kept going further, demonstrating the independent spirit that is also typical of "alternative New York." He founded his production company 40 Acres and a Mule Filmworks, which has studios and offices in the eclectic and happening neighborhoods of Fort Greene and DUMBO (an acronym for Down Under the Manhattan Bridge Overpass).

Red Hook
Graffiti are often to be seen on the house walls and balustrades of Brooklyn. The ones shown here, situated in the former port zone of Red Hook, have a strong social content.

"Today DUMBO is gentrified, but it's still an interesting area
to explore, full of new trends, and still populated by artists
and creative people going to art exhibitions,
live music and many cultural events."

An antiques shop in the heart of **DUMBO**.
A café in **DUMBO** with an eclectic and artistic atmosphere.

DUMBO is full of art galleries and artists' lofts. It is home to the DUMBO Arts Center and DUMBO Arts Festival, bookshops, coffee shops and restaurants. And it contains a popular and beautiful park overlooking the East River, the panoramic terrace of Fulton Ferry Landing and State Park.

DUMBO used to be a manufacturing district, full of warehouses and factories that made machinery, paper boxes and soap pads. But, since the de-industrialization of the 1970s, it has started becoming residential and artistic, both bohemian and urban, with many artists who moved here in search of inexpensive loft apartments. "Today DUMBO is gentrified," Lee explains. "But it's still an interesting area to explore, full of new trends, and still populated by artists and creative people going to art exhibitions, live music and many cultural events."

Despite the relative coldness – for his Brooklyn outsider spirit – of Manhattan's Upper East Side, Spike Lee enjoys the historical part of his new neighborhood and gravitates to its "institutions", like the local coffee shop in Yorkville, called Viand. "It's on 78st and Madison Avenue and I think it's one of the best places to get a good coffee in New York."

"New York is in me. It's part of my blood and my soul,
and in my movies I've tried to represent its different aspects."

With the eye of an artist and a great filmmaker, he has been discovering one of the most evocative parts of the Upper East Side in his beautiful film, *25th Hour*, based on the novel *The 25th Hour* by David Benioff. "There is a scene where Edward Norton sits with his dog on a park bench in Carl Schurz Park, one of most romantic places in the City," he says. The park overlooks the waters of Hell Gate and Wards Island in the East River. Its stunning waterfront promenade, winding shady paths, green lawns and flowers are a favorite for dog owners and locals. Also, on the site, sits Gracie Mansion, built for Archibald Gracie in 1799, and which is now the official residence of the Mayor of New York.

DUMBO Arts Center
Posters that have been transformed into artistic works at the DUMBO Arts Center, which organizes modern and contemporary art shows and is the hub of the autumn DUMBO Arts Festival.

Art in DUMBO
Founded in 1997, the DUMBO Arts Center has played a fundamental role in making this neighborhood a premier cultural district and tourist attraction.

The facade and an aerial view of **Madison Square Garden**.

"My New York is the one of the New York Knicks basketball team playing in Madison Square Garden."

But, to get to know Spike Lee's New York you must also open up to one of the City's most popular traditions – sports. "New York is all about sports. They create such a great sense of belonging and community," he explains, with his great passion for sports. "My New York is the one of the New York Knicks basketball team playing in Madison Square Garden, the New York Yankees baseball team, the Giants and the Jets in football." And so, in the 2009 documentary *Kobe Doin' Work*, Lee chose to focus on a day in the life of the basketball player Kobe Bryant.

"My father gave me his love of the world of sport, as well as music," says Lee. "From him I inherited a passion for baseball, basketball, tennis, soccer, and football. Sport has a special meaning for me, and it's bound up in that connection with my father. Now, I'm teaching it to my son, who's into soccer, baseball and ice hockey, and it's like a cycle that comes around," he muses. "Sport unites souls, leads you to celebrate and suffer together, just like life, and like New York. I strongly believe that sport is part of the New York soul."

DANIEL LIBESKIND

The "Visionary" of the City

A man is his visions, his ideas. This is even stronger for an architect like Daniel Libeskind, whose work can shape the profile of a City. "New York is a Utopia of thoughts, where dreams and ideas can become true. New York has always loved big thinkers and made them part of its soul, its life and its people," he says. "New York adopts their talents, and their humanity. Their feelings and sensitivities have become part of its rich and varied spirit."

Daniel Libeskind's ideas have influenced a whole generation of architects and anyone interested in the future of cities and culture. Libeskind is not only an architect and artist. His work is a stream of different notes that illuminate the skyline like a visual melody, and his vision is part of the future of the City.

"I was a professional musician and I love music. I can't live without it, and I like to listen to it and make it go deeply into my soul," he says. "In the end, music is very similar to architecture. They are both quite abstract, they are both 'written' in a very special way, each vibration can't be out by even a microtone. Music is architecturally organized on a piece of paper, and it has to be represented by a large choir or orchestra. It is, for an audience, like architecture," he reflects. "As an architect and creator of projects, I am not only the one playing the piano or the cello, but I must direct and conduct

> New York is architecture and music, like an immense kaleidoscope of sounds and forms, floating high in the sky.

my architecture as an abstract and intellectual piece of music. New York is architecture and music, like an immense kaleidoscope of sounds and forms, floating high in the sky, and which you can admire from different points of view, changing the perspective at the slightest movement."

For this visionary, "Music communicates the deepest desire of the soul in emotions, like architecture. Music transforms. We are transformed by a piece of music in a way very similar to architecture. It's not only about numbers, statistics, mathematical calculations, and new technologies. It is about the human experience of the human being. It is a question of being there to be transformed and open to the different possibilities of the world," he says, commenting on the deep connection between the architecture and the music of New York.

"I love all musical genres, ancient, classical, pop, rock, rap, blues and jazz, and Jewish music from the temple, and New York has all of them. I'm fascinated by Bach's world, as he is a marvelous 'architect.' I studied his music and, among the notes, he creates messages for the future. That is what I try to create with my architecture. New York, for me, with all the different forms of architecture that make the City, represents a symphony of music where I can try to play my part."

Daniel Libeskind was born in the Republic of Poland in 1946, to Jewish parents who were Holocaust survivors. An immigrant to America, with his family, he became an American citizen in 1964. He studied music in Israel and New York, and became a virtuoso performer but, eventually, dedicated himself to the study of architecture, earning a degree, in 1970, from New York City's Cooper Union for the Advancement of Science and Art, and a Masters Degree in the History and Theory of Architecture from the University of Essex in Great Britain in 1971.

Throughout his career he has worked all over the world, keeping studios initially in Berlin, then Zurich and Milan as well as Manhattan, but there is a deep bond that connects him to New York. "New York is a large public space in the open air. New York is one open space, with infinite horizons. New York is a city where people love living together, without religious boundaries and cultural limitations. People from all over the world arrive here with a dream. New York is a city without borders," he says. His work, which has been described as deconstructive, also embodies the revolutionary spirit of the City.

Libeskind was selected to manifest his vision of New York in one of his masterpieces, the Master Plan Redevelopment of the World Trade Center, destroyed in the September 11, 2001 terror attacks. "As a young architect student, I watched the original World Trade Center being built in the 1960s, my father was working in a print shop on Stone Street in Lower Manhattan.

Rebirth
This photograph of the 9/11 Memorial Park reflected in the wall of another building was taken while the new World Trade Center was still being constructed.

Freedom Tower

Detail of the perfect form and architectural proportions of the Freedom Tower. It is 541 meters or 1776 feet tall. The Freedom Tower, also known as One World Trade Center, dominates the surrounding skyscrapers. Construction of the building took seven years (2004-2013).

"My vision of the new Master Plan for the World Trade Center is for it to be, first, for people. For me it is important that it is a place for Memory and a place where people can meet and spend time together. I think that architecture has a central role in doing something positive, in creating something that shows we are together and that we are New Yorkers. This offers me great inspiration," he points out.

"I am so lucky to be an architect in New York," Libeskind believes, "There is something so unique, fantastic and magical here that gives me wonderful ideas. New York is like an old 'cathedral' of American architecture to me. Like so many people, I love New York. With all its vibrant power, it's the center of the world. And, for me personally, it's the city of inspiration in every sense. Inspiration comes from everywhere here – from people walking on the sidewalk, from looking someone in the eye, from the love that's in the air, from an accident of fate. You are inspired by everything!"

"New York is a Utopia of thoughts, where dreams and ideas can become true. New York has always loved big thinkers and made them part of its soul, its life and its people."

Hearst Tower, home of the famous mass media Hearst Corporation.
The **skyscrapers of Manhattan** reflect one another.

With deep feeling for the City, Libeskind also remembers his heritage. "I am an immigrant, and here in New York I have felt at home since the beginning. But New York also reminds one of a history that we should never forget, as here everything and everybody is deeply connected. There's always something unexpected happening here to make you suddenly stop and think."

The new WTC project has brought together a creative team of international architects, artists and urban developers with the vision to create a grand, new urban center for a 21st century New York – now, more than ever, a Capital of the World. The entire "Memory Foundations" Master Plan, conceived by Libeskind, includes four new skyscrapers. 1WTC, named the Freedom Tower by Governor Pataki and initially designed by Libeskind, was then re-designed by David Childs, while 2WTC came from the minds of architects Foster and Partners. The 3WTC construction was developed by Richard Rogers, and 4WTC is a vision by Fumihiko Maki and Associates. The result is an incredible center, redefining Lower Manhattan and its skyline with ideas coming from all over the world, which, according to Libeskind, "reflects the New York melting pot."

There are other elements in the World Trade Center that he conceives as a huge "piazza."

The National September 11 Memorial Museum, designed by Davis Brody Bond, is a spectacular underground space below the Memorial Plaza and incorporates the Slurry Wall into the structure. The entrance visitor center is designed by Snohetta.

Reflecting Absence, by Michael Arad, stands as its emotional heart, with a forest of trees and two square pools in the middle where the Twin Towers once stood. On the edges of the Memorial pools there are the names of all the victims. The World Trade Center Transportation Hub, PATH, by Santiago Calatrava, resembles a bird taking off into the sky. It is a symbol of hope and of the future toward which the City always aims. The new WTC is like a playful game of various different ideas, coexisting in a peaceful dream like the multitude of people and nationalities in New York.

"When they asked Goethe his favorite color he answered, 'the rainbow'," says Libeskind. "It is very difficult to choose the most beautiful buildings in New York, as I love too many of them: ancient, modern, sacred, commercial ones, churches and cathedrals, townhouses and brownstones, small houses and apartments. They are all connected in a beautiful and unique world."

"Each building has a special idea inside it.

A Play of Forms
The skyscraper with the head offices of *The New York Times*, designed by Renzo Piano, is the fourth tallest building in the city.

137

Contemporary architecture is to be seen almost everywhere in Manhattan.
Beekman Tower, designed by Frank Gehry.

"I am so lucky to be an architect in New York, there is something so unique, fantastic and magical here that gives me wonderful ideas."

"It hides art behind it, but also creation, love and pain. What I love most about architecture in New York is that it is the public art of a city.

"It has its own pure beauty that communicates, democratically, to everybody. New York is becoming a better city, because it's creating more and more public and cultural spaces for everybody, making people feel even closer," says the architect, on his vision of the City.

Daniel Libeskind believes that "New York should not just be a 'private playground' for rich people. It must guarantee places to live and work to everybody. This is the only way to guarantee that its incredible energy can stay alive. This will make of New York an even a more marvelous and pluralistic city."

"I always remember what the Statue of Liberty represents – the eternal hope of immigrants like me. It says that, even if you are tired and poor, you deserve to be free. Like never before," believes the visionary architect, "New York is going through a Renaissance and rising from its ashes."

Winter Colors
The Manhattan skyline, here dominated by the Freedom Tower, in winter, when the contrast and intensity of colors create a spectacular image.

STEVE McCURRY

The "Photographer" of the City

You can find Steve McCurry in the desert with a camera in hand, capturing a dust storm or passengers sitting atop an overcrowded bus. What he is most known for, though, is his photograph of Sharbat Gula, the green-eyed "Afghan Girl" that made the cover of *National Geographic's* June 1985 issue. Despite the fact that he is always traveling for work, you can find him in New York, as it is the place he calls home.

"I live across the street from Washington Square Park. I have spent many hours there over the years photographing, reading, and relaxing. I feel truly at home there," he confesses. "I love life, different kinds of people, some of whom are reading, sleeping, playing chess or music, or running around with their dogs. This park is best during the summer, when there are many performances."

Born in Pennsylvania, Steve remembers the first time he came to New York. "When I visited New York, in 1964, with my family, we went to the World's Fair in Queens. I recall being overwhelmed by the buildings and crowds and the pace of life seemed to be very fast," he says. "We went to the Empire State Building. I was amazed by its colossal structure – my breath was completely taken away. I remember the profound view and the enormity of the landscape, which was quite different from the Pennsylvanian suburbs where I spent my childhood. It was in the evening that I began seeing the lights of this vibrant city at sunset. The blue of the sky was becoming illuminated by the lights that were switching on in the windows and in the streets."

Steve McCurry is one of the most recognized photographers of the 21st century, with his evident compassion toward humanity. What makes him a New Yorker is that his images are rich with subjects that reveal the authentic spirit of the city. His photography has been a constant, and never ending, journey. He explains when he first became fascinated with documenting his surroundings. "I was 22 years old and studying film at university when I was attracted to photography. I took several fine art photography classes and photographed for the university's newspaper. I realized that all I needed was a camera to explore the world, and see things from another perspective," he says.

"When I was 19, I spent a year in Europe living in Stockholm and Amsterdam and later, when I was 22, I went to Central America and spent several months in Africa. Initially, traveling for pleasure, and then work, became imbued with the purpose of discovering different worlds and cultures.

> New York has a bit of a gray quality, with its bursts of yellow-orange from the cabs. That's how I see New York.

The shadow of the Empire State Building hovers over Midtown.
The Chrysler Building and Empire State Building, architectural icons of the city.

"... the Empire State Building.
I was amazed by its colossal structure,
my breath was completely taken away."

"At 25, I started to work for a newspaper, after which I lived in India for two years. India was an incredible discovery for me, a world full of exotic colors and religions. That is where I met amazing people, encountered new cultures, and learned more about Buddhism, Hinduism, Jainism, and Sikhism," he adds. "Having photographed in Asia, one realizes that there exists a different pace, a different life from what we in the West are used to. Being a modern society, our focus tends to be all about speed and results, but it is humbling to know that there are more pressing concerns that people have to worry about. Those are situations where I find inspiration and want to take pictures to reveal the souls of such people to the world, but also in New York. Photographs can tell profound stories," he explains.

His images reveal the truth of New York, in a way that is unique to his artistry and to the city itself. He conveys intimacy in the moments of ordinary life, creating a sense of surrealism amongst his subjects.

His New York is at once intimate and real. Every single time he takes a picture, his novel manner of viewing the city is evident. His images are a sequence of unexpected stories and moments, or when the moment becomes history, such as 9/11. "Certainly 9/11 was one of the most shocking, disturbing, and incredible days. It's still hard to describe in words. I had just returned from an assignment in China the previous day. Something about the magnitude of 3,000 innocent people from different nationalities being massacred, it was such an insane and brutal attack. In my photos at Ground Zero, I tried to show the heroism and nobility of the people of New York City," he remembers.

Steve still likes the more authentic New York, the one where you can run into interesting people. "I love Greenwich Village. When I first arrived here, it was a different planet, because of the people, how they were dressed, how they were acting in different ways, the many coffee shops, and the behavior of quite bizarre characters. It was as if everybody was living on the street. I came from a small town in Pennsylvania, and in Washington Square Park there were artists playing and singing, so many people full of colors. I did not want to go home again, I had no interest in it at all," he recalls. "At first, I lived in SoHo, when it was the hub of the artistic community. I was living on Sullivan Street, a place that today is a great restaurant location.

The Empire State Building
The grandiose skyscraper is reflected on another building, creating a surprising effect. When Steve McCurry was on the observation deck he was bewitched by the city lights.

"At that time, in the middle 1970s, I decided to do a workshop, a photo project with a friend about the stories of people in the street.

"Homeless people have always fascinated me the most in New York. I remember this woman with her shopping cart, who looked like she was crazy; she was probably schizophrenic – very poor. She was around Columbus Circle. When I talked to her, though, she had amazing stories to tell; she had fallen on tough circumstances. Her husband had died and she got sick, lost her job and ended up like that," he recalls.

"Today, I still love Greenwich Village. One of my favorite neighborhoods is the Bowery, where a friend of mine has an amazing building that is eight stories high. He owns it and he lives at the top. I like the atmosphere of the area – it's still a bit underground, where you can find graffiti on the walls," he says. "Since I travel a lot, when I'm back in New York, I like to spend time working in my studio. When I'm not at the studio, I go to the movies at the Angelika Film Center, or meet friends for dinner Downtown. I like to go to Souen, a macrobiotic restaurant in New York, or to Café Regio for a coffee, or to McSorley's in the East Village for a drink and where you can meet a lot of intriguing individuals."

Another place that inspires him is Grand Central Station. The ceiling with its art work, the grand, elegant halls, suggesting a building from another time. "I used my last roll of Kodachrome there, with which I also photographed Robert De Niro," he adds.

Leisure
In his spare time Steve McCurry often goes to the Angelika Film Center, which offers a program of independent and foreigner directors.

"Every photographer has a different source of inspiration. New York is one of the most significant cities in the world, as it is a melting pot of people from all walks of life and cultures from around the world."

"The city, to my mind, has a strong and compelling energy.
Everyone is here with a sense of purpose –
out to find themselves and make a mark professionally,
which greatly defines its momentum and pace."

Paintings, drawings and photos at the **McSorley's Old Ale House**.

Central Park is always a special location for him too. "It is unique with its ice skating rink, lakes, bridges, and rocks. Fall, with its foliage, is my favorite time of the year, but I like walking in the solitude of the snow, when not many other people are walking around," he says.

Steve McCurry's New York is beautiful, uplifting, and affecting. It reveals itself with the special eye of the great artist he is, with his sensibility that goes deeply in the colors and the soul of city life, in the intimacy of the unguarded moment.

"New York has a bit of a gray quality, with its bursts of yellow-orange from the cabs. That's how I see New York. I generally work in cloudy, overcast conditions when the light is more even and there is less contrast. Thanks to the tall buildings, ample shade and shadows, this is the perfect place for me to shoot."

"My best photograph in New York? My photograph of Times Square at evening, when it was snowing. It was very cold and dark. It was amazing. It was around 5:30 pm in the afternoon and a lot of people were there, among lights, signs and traffic, typical of the city."

His Favorite Haunt
Steve McCurry prefers to go to characteristic places like the McSorley's Old Ale House, which is filled with artworks, antiques, and vintage bric-a-brac that take one backward in time.

151

The four-face clock in the main hall of **Grand Central Terminal**.

New York is an infinite source of inspiration to him. "Every photographer has a different source of inspiration. New York is one of the most significant cities in the world, as it is a melting pot of people from all walks of life and cultures from around the world. A lot of esteemed photographers have photographed in New York, and I don't think it's more arduous to photograph here than any other place," he states.

"The city, to my mind, has a strong and compelling energy. Everyone is here with a sense of purpose – out to find themselves and make a mark professionally, which greatly defines its momentum and pace," he concludes. "The reality is that it is difficult to make it anywhere in the world. I believe that New York offers a lot more opportunities, thus making it easier. However, along with more opportunities comes a lot more competition, but if you have to compete with the best, there is no better arena in which to do so."

Grand Central Terminal
The facade of the world's largest railway station by number of platforms. GCT is another symbol of New York. Behind it is another city icon, the MetLife Building.

JAY McINERNEY

The "Eyes" of the City

The eye of a writer is different from that of anyone else. Characters emerge from people he meets or from a unique snippet of street life. They become real, first in his mind and then on the page. A writer's eye develops a particular sensitivity from the art of constantly playing and fighting with words.

A writer lives in his own world, but Jay McInerney has the courage to go beyond that. He watches and listens, taking an active role in the New York scene and city life, while his words tell, in real time, the perpetual tale of a vibrant and ever-transforming metropolis.

"My secret," McInerney confides, "is that I observe. I scrutinize the lives of New Yorkers and what they do around me. New York is a platform for me to portray people and their stories. I try to understand the nuances of a certain behavior or action. I explore different worlds: the financial sector, literary and artistic worlds, philanthropic organizations, young people and students, or high society charity events, bars, the night club scene, the buzz of New York, the flight and despair of many souls in search of life's meaning."

In New York, he believes, "most people still live to prove they can belong to a particular clique or social class."

> I scrutinize the lives of New Yorkers and what they do around me. New York is a platform for me to portray people and their stories.

McInerney is a New York insider who knows all of its neighborhoods with their secrets and social strata. Having lived in nearly all of them, for one reason or another, and thoroughly explored the others, Jay McInerney is the "eyes" of a New York that he reveals in each page of his novels. Much of his work is autobiographically inspired, and you can discover New York in it.

His first novel, *Bright Lights, Big City*, "chronicles the New York face: the lives of struggling young people and the struggle for success of a young writer working as a fact-checker for *The New Yorker* to support himself, as I also once did," he said. In the book, he describes the world of fashion models, cocaine, sex, nightlife, and the excesses of the 1980s, not so different from today. "And this is also New York, a sprawling monster of irresistible temptations with its classes and their habits, as if they were a tribe," he adds.

In his other novels, we discover even more about different New York eras. They are variously inspired by the 9/11 terrorist attack and the sense of community that developed in New York in its wake, or by his many marriages (such as his most recent to heiress Anne Hearst, also a figure of New York City history), by high society and tradition, the Wall Street Crash, his experience of

"Skyscrapers have always been very beautiful to me, like the mountains and canyons of the City. I could spend hours gazing at the structure of the Empire State Building or the Chrysler."

fatherhood, the world of culture and intellectuals, or the beautiful women who are eternally part of the fun side of the City, and the renaissance of contemporary New York, with the new WTC. "New York is a place where people do not think of the past, only of the present and of the future," he points out.

Story of My Life, *Model Behavior*, *The Good Life*, and *How It Ended*, a collection of short stories, each offers a love letter to his beloved city. While Jay is himself part of New York, he is also its chronicler. With an uncannily objective eye, he is capable of painting a remarkable literary portrait of the City – a mirror image in 3D. Reading his work, you can touch, smell and feel those things and those people. He seduces with writing that is as enchanting as the City's lights.

"When I arrived in New York, the city was dirty and decrepit, but it had a certain flair that now I miss. It was the metropolitan frontier, the Urban Wild West," he observes. "It was full of graffiti. It was dangerous and you had to watch your back," he continued.

"But, as I said, I kind of miss all of that. I miss that colorful and underground spirit, now that everything's so clean and nice.

Empire State Building
The Empire State Building, built in 1901 in the Art Deco style, boasts one of the most famous panoramic terraces in the world, with the best views of the city.

Flatiron Building
View of the Flatiron Building, with its characteristic triangular shape. Jay McInerney has always been fascinated by the profile of his city's high-rises.

The stairway and the glass cube of the **Apple Store** on 5th Avenue.

"New York is a place where people do not think of the past, only of the present and of the future."

"Recently, I saw some graffiti again in the Lower East Side and, as soon as I see one, I try to take a photo of it with my iPhone. Because, for me, New York is the spirit of graffiti in how it can live through moments that are so colorful, beautiful, marvelous, and sometimes deep, but which can easily vanish – and just like graffiti that gets washed off, be forgotten in the City's burning desire to look ahead."

Jay recalls the atmosphere of New York in the 1980s. "It was an era when people were starting to get rich. I saw the same people lose everything and then make it back. New York is the place of cycles of ups and downs, of psychological and materialistic shifts," he explains, admitting that

he knows "what it means to have money and then not to have it," and observing that "despite being the most beautiful and interesting place in the world, New York is risky, challenging, and perilous."

Jay McInerney was born in Hartford, Connecticut in 1955 and studied writing with the iconic writer Raymond Carver, before moving to Manhattan, before becoming famous and emerging, in the 1980s, as one of the "Brat Pack", which included Bret Easton Ellis, and struggling hard. "It was not that easy, but I can say that I have been lucky. I made it. And even when I had no money, I was always very happy in the City," he recalls.

Top of the Rocks, the panoramic terrace of Rockefeller Center.

"Skyscrapers have always been very beautiful to me, like the mountains and canyons of the City. I could spend hours gazing at the structure of the Empire State Building or the Chrysler," explains the writer. "In the last ten years the cityscape has been redrawn. Some new buildings are beautiful, like the works of Richard Meier or Frank Gehry, and others are horrible," he says. "In all honesty, as long as I can remember nearly nobody liked the World Trade Center until it collapsed. From New York, I've learned to see the irony in every tragedy."

As far as neighborhoods are concerned, McInerney loves Greenwich Village, where he has lived in many apartments throughout his life. "Now I have a penthouse in the vicinity of Washington Square Park. It's in an old art deco building with doorman. It also has terraces, which are very difficult to find in New York, and in one of them I have a Japanese garden," he says.

Futuristic Architecture
The address of the avant-garde Bank of America Tower (2009) is One Bryant Park, which is the name often given to the bank.

Sunset at **Central Park** toward Midtown.

Jay has always found this neighborhood fascinating, "and it's certainly my favorite," he says. "In the 1920s and even earlier, artists and writers like Eugene O'Neill, Marianne Moore, Jackson Pollock, and Willem de Kooning lived here." When I moved to New York for the first time, I had this romantic image of the city, and back then in the 1980s it was still bohemian. There were no bankers or Wall Street traders living here," he remembers. "I lived in the neighborhood when I wrote *Bright Lights, Big City* so it's no coincidence that the protagonist lives just along West 12th Street. It's in a building where I've never lived but which I liked enough to choose as the backdrop for my book."

"Now it's become expensive," McInerney observes. "But the neighborhood has kept its character, thanks to New York University and its surrounding student life. I have always loved student districts," he confides. "It makes me feel alive to have so many young people around."

How has New York changed now? "The districts of New York were divided into 'tribes.' In the Upper East Side there were the Germans, in Chinatown the Chinese, in Little Italy the Italians, while around Central Park people were very wealthy," Jay says. "The West Side was the theater district, where many actors lived, and the Upper West Side was very Jewish. The sense of neighborhood is still strong, but people are more mixed now and the differences are no longer so clearly marked."

George Washington Bridge
The bridge connecting Manhattan Washington Heights and Fort Lee, New Jersey was inaugurated in 1931 and is one of the busiest bridges in the world.

> "New York always changes; it's a mistake to believe it will ever remain the same, because that's not possible. New buildings, people, business, and a continuous incessant movement: this is New York."

There are quite a few places where Jay McInerney likes to go in New York: "There are restaurants I mention in my books like The Odeon or Raoul's, which are part of the New York scene. But there are other places I also like a lot, like 21 Club, where I celebrated my marriage to Anne Hearst, or Gotham Bar and Grill, the Spotted Pig, Babbo, Waverly Inn, and Minetta Tavern. New York is also a City of restaurants, a temple for the foodie and those who want to try the best gastronomy and cuisine from all over the world, with the enchanting spices and tastes of master chefs experimenting with new and different flavors. Actually, in New York I could write a list of a hundred restaurants, and each week they open another good one!" he declares. "But I prefer restaurants that stand the test of time; places that, just like people, have a story to tell."

What's his New York motto? "I'm an optimist and a hopeless romantic: Eat, Drink, Love, and Remarry."

In addition to his love of women, Jay is an epicurean. He loves the good life, good wine, and he loves to eat. He wrote a wine column for *House & Garden* magazine and now writes one for the *Wall Street Journal* and has published books like *Bacchus and Me: Adventures in the Wine Cellar,*

A Hedonist in the Cellar: Adventures in Wine, and *The Juice: Vinous Veritas.*

What does he see for the future of New York? "New York always changes; it's a mistake to believe it will ever remain the same, because that's not possible. New buildings, people, business, and a continuous incessant movement: this is New York," he explains. "The tragedy of 9/11 created a great sense of community among people, and yet now almost nobody speaks too much of that day. I can see the Freedom Tower now from my apartment, and a new New York has been growing all these years from its ashes."

View from the **panoramic terrace** of the Empire State Building.

The Manhattan **skyline** in the late evening.

The **Queensboro Bridge** passes over Roosevelt Island.

MOBY

The "Sound" of the City

Moby is one of the world's most famous electronic singer-songwriters, musicians and DJs, but he is also a great artist and photographer. His artistry is revealed in his vision of New York City. "New York is so iconic that you can recognize it even from a photograph that is a bit out of focus from the window of a taxi, covered with rain drops. It is just a short glimpse of it, but you can see what it is immediately. So I looked and shot," he says, talking about one photo that he took coming back from one of his music tours. It is a rare and unique image of the Empire State Building from the window of a taxi ride from Queens to Manhattan.

Moby is a multi-talented artist and creator, a genius in many artistic forms, able to reach immediately into your soul or, as he states, to make you feel uncomfortable with yourself, to provoke a reaction in you, able to make you reflect. And he is a New Yorker, even if he has been spending recent years living in LA. But it has been New York that inspired his creative process, where it all started for him and where he always returns, rediscovering his home through new eyes, the lens of a camera or a succession of sounds and words.

Moby was born in Harlem, the son of a medical secretary and a chemistry professor, and his middle name and nickname is "Moby," given to him by his parents because of an ancestral relation to *Moby Dick* author Herman Melville, who was his great-great-great-grand uncle. "I grew up in New York. It was where I was born; it was where I grew up in the 1970s and I thought that it was the strangest and weirdest place in the world," he remembers. "All my favorite writers, musicians and artists lived there, and it was so dirty and exciting and dangerous. When I was a kid, when I was 14-15 years old, in the Lower East Side, I found New York the best place to be – wild and adventurous with the strangest bars and clubs. New York in the 1980s was so odd and dynamic. The artists, the writers, the musicians, the designers, everybody was hanging out together, and I could experience music of all genres. And then, in the 1990s, it became cleaner and it was not as bad. It was safer, but it lost something. Some people thought that the gentrification was stopping at some point, but it did not," he says.

Moby has been influenced by the sounds of New York City, and he has created his own sound. He has been mixing different genres like blues, soul, rock, techno, breakbeat hardcore, electronica, dance and house. He has sold over 20 million albums worldwide, created masterpieces like *Play, 18, Hotel, Go, the very best of Moby, Last Night, Wait for Me, Destroyed, Innocents,*

> Everything in New York provokes an opposite reaction that is, in the end, a quest of immense creativity!

The **Blue Condominium** by Bernard Tschumi in the Lower East Side.
A mural advertising an Asian restaurant in the **Lower East Side**.

"New York is so iconic that you can recognize it even from
a photograph that is a bit out of focus from the window of a taxi,
covered with rain drops. It is just a short glimpse of it,
but you can see what it is immediately."

singles like *Lift Me Up* and *Natural Blues* that are part of daily life, and soundtracks for movies like the James Bond film *Tomorrow Never Dies* (1997), Michael Mann's film *Heat* (1995), *Southland Tales* (2006), and others.

He has co-written, produced and remixed music for many other famous artists such as David Bowie, Michael Jackson, The Pet Shop Boys, Britney Spears, Public Enemy, Guns N' Roses, Metallica, and Soundgarden. His album *Last Night*, in

particular, is a kind of "feeling of the City" with a deep touch. Released in 2008, it is an eclectic album of electronic dance music inspired by a night out in his New York neighborhood of the Lower East Side. "I recorded that album in my studio on the Lower East Side. I wanted to do something very personal, I wanted to record everything at home by myself," he confesses.

"The creative inspiration behind the record was hearing a David Lynch speech at BAFTA, in the UK.

A project by Shanzhai Biennial at the **MoMA PS1**.

> "When I think about how New York has influenced me,
> I believe it is how it has exposed me to music that
> I would have not heard in a small suburb."

He is a friend of mine now, and we have collaborated on many projects. Then he was talking about creativity and how good it can be without market pressure. So, in making this record I wanted to focus on something that I loved, without being concerned about how it might be received by the marketplace. It is quieter, more melodic and personal than anything else I made in the past," he says.

New York City inspires Moby from a visual point of view, as well as through its sounds. As a photographer in New York he is represented by the Emmanuel Fremin Gallery, 547 West 27th Street, in Chelsea, which organizes different exhibitions of his work. In his photographic book *Destroyed* (2011), together with his album, he shot images that feature the contrast of being isolated in empty spaces, like dressing rooms or hotel rooms before a concert, and in front of a crowd during a concert. "I have been taking photographs since I was 10 years old, and I grew up around film and darkrooms. My uncle, Joseph Kugielsky, was a photographer for *The New York Times*, and I have always found that his job was amazing," he says.

His photos, taken in New York, are very personal and unique, full of his artistic sensitivity and desire to provoke.

Art in Queens
An exhibition of works by John Miller at the MoMA PS1. Affiliated to the Museum of Modern Art since 2000, the PS1 is one of the leading American institutions dedicated to contemporary art.

A **street in Chinatown** during a snowstorm.
Merchandise arriving at a **stall in a street** in Chinatown.

Among them, there is one of the sky over Newark Airport at night, as if it was a wasted place in the middle of some faraway universe. One is of La Guardia Airport, which is the book cover as well. It is a candid, long white corridor and at the top is a sign with the word "DESTROYED." "In fact, there was a sign saying all unattended luggage will be destroyed, and I waited till only the last word could be seen on the display. But I do not want to explain my art too much, I think that the artist is there to create and to provoke questions, a discussion, or a reaction. I prefer to create a level so that the viewer has to respond," he says. "Music is a very temporary, defined art form like film.

"In order to experience music you have to listen to it in a way that it has been written. In photography, and visual art in general, the viewer decides the relationship of it, you get closer and you get far away, as you want. There is a democracy that I appreciate," he reflects.

"In 2009, I decided I was ready to have a change from New York and so I went to LA, even though I keep coming and going. New York is always my home and the place where I come from.

"I had been living in my own apartment in the Lower East Side since the 1980s, and then I was living on 96th Street and Central Park West," he adds. "In New York now I like Long Island, which is still very urban, and then Chinatown in that part where Canal Street goes on and on to where it meets Orchard Street. I still feel like a foreigner here.

"I grew up in New York and I thought that
it was the strangest and weirdest place
in the world."

"I like strange places that do not make sense," he explains. "When I am in New York, as I am a veteran vegan and an animal activist, I like to go to Angelika Kitchen, 300 E 12th Street, a vegetarian restaurant in the East Village. When I come back it is the first place I go, one of the few places in the big City that you have the feeling they will never change," he says.

"When I think about how New York has influenced me, I believe it is how it has exposed me to music that I would have not heard in a small suburb. My parents were Protestant, and they were listening to folk and classical music, which I love too, but New York exposed me to different kinds of music, black music, African music, hip hop, Arabic and Latino music, R&B, all styles of urban music that did not come from my world heritage," he reflects. "That is because my music is so different," he adds. "Also, if you think of the big influence New York can have, it is funny, as it is very often an opposing influence. If you think of the Guggenheim Museum – at the time it was created it was inspired by New York, but it was going in the other direction architecture-wise. It was an 'anti-New York building' compared to other buildings around it. A lot of urban architecture, design and music is inspired by the City, but also opposite to the City," he thinks. "New York is very loud and so when you are out in the City, you feel the need, as an artist, to go home and have a quiet environment. So, I create a calm refuge in the face of chaos where I am able to develop my art. Everything in New York provokes an opposite reaction that is, in the end, a quest of immense creativity!"

Night Colors
Standing out behind the Manhattan Bridge is the unmistakable shape of the Empire State Building, which at night is illuminated with lights of different colors.

ROBERT AND CORTNEY NOVOGRATZ

The "Designers" of the City

Robert and Cortney Novogratz are two of the most renowned interior designers in New York, as well as being art collectors and philanthropists, and beloved by many celebrities.

New York is a kaleidoscopic rainbow of forms and colors. And they can shape them, reinvent them, and discover them in a beautiful piece of old furniture or rediscover the sensuality and cool spirit of New York in masterpieces of modern art. With their seven children, and known for their marvelous parties, like the one they usually throw for Halloween, they have been called "the coolest family in the world" by *The Times* of London, and they are known to millions worldwide through their unique lifestyle, design aesthetic and TV programs. Their first show, *9 by Design*, aired on Bravo, and their show, *Home by Novogratz* on HGTV, have been two of the networks' most popular programs.

But first of all, they are, and feel themselves to be, New Yorkers, because they have a special and romantic connection to the City and they have been living here for many years, even if, these days, they also spend a lot of time in Los Angeles. "Robert proposed to me on a snowy night on the top of the Empire State Building. I have always loved New York in the snow, and afterwards we had drinks in The Oak Room at The Plaza Hotel," says Cortney.

What is their feeling for New York? "New York is, and will always be, the greatest city in the world. There is no other place that has the energy that you can find in this place," adds Robert. "When you fly back home to New York, you feel it is your city, the best city. And when you land, you realize lots of people probably feel the same way."

> When you fly back home to New York, you feel it is your city, the best city. And when you land, you realize lots of people probably feel the same way.

Robert grew up in Alexandria, Virginia, and Cortney in southern Georgia. They were both from large families, and they both inherited their love for their creative jobs from their parents, who were decorating enthusiasts. They met in Charlotte, North Carolina, and decided to move to New York to work in the design world. At first, Robert and his brother Michael were athletes and enjoyed many sports. But he shared another incredible passion with Cortney – the arts. "Our style mixes together old and new, vintage and contemporary art," explains Cortney. "I take care more of the furniture and Robert of the art, but we have the same taste."

"I will never choose a piece that she does not like," he points out. And New York has always been a great place for inspiration and possibilities for them.

They began their career by renovating run-down properties in Manhattan, like 5 Centre Market Place, in SoHo, converted from a former gun shop, and other properties in the area along Thompson Street. In 2009, they also published their first book, *Downtown Chic.*

"When we moved to New York, over twenty years ago, we just wanted our homes to be reflections of who we were," explains Robert. "New York is not for everyone. It is a place you can come to and create an amazing life. You can start from nothing and the sky really is the limit. This is why people from all over the world still move here every day. New York is an amazing place, but it is the people of the City which make it so unique."

What do they like most about the City? "We love that New York is a walking city," says Robert. "We enjoy going to Madison Square Garden, watching the Macy's Thanksgiving Day Parade, eating pizza and hot dogs from street vendors," he says. "We enjoy the characters of the city, taking in a Broadway show, cheering on runners in the NYC Marathon, celebrating at the Halloween parade, and enjoy the change of seasons, especially the fall. We don't like that it is becoming homogenized like everywhere else."

Central Park in Winter
This enthralling aerial view of Upper Manhattan, with the Bronx in the background, shows Central Park covered with snow.

"We love that New York is a walking city."

The **New York Marathon**.

"New York is really an amazing place for kids."

Regarding their favorite places in the City, they also have a very clear sense of it. "We are Downtown people - our family has lived in SoHo for 15 years, and for five years in the West Village," states Robert. "We go to local places like Felix, Arturo's Pizza, Raoul's and the Lure Fish Bar. We love hanging out at The Crosby Street Hotel and at The Mercer. As a family, we love to go antiquing to places like Mantiques, Paula Rubenstein and Adelaide. They are our faves. We really like Flavor Paper in Brooklyn, ABC Carpet & Home, shopping at What Goes Around Comes Around for vintage clothes, and our kids love Uncle Funky's Boards."

Living in the City with all their kids has been a great experience that has showed them how New York can also be a family place. "All our seven kids were born at Lenox Hill Hospital and are true New Yorkers.

Parade Balloons
The Thanksgiving Day Parade is famous for its gigantic balloons representing famous and fantasy personalities that move among the City's tall buildings.

"New York is not for everyone.
It is a place you can come to and create
an amazing life. You can start from nothing
and the sky really is the limit."

They enjoy playing basketball at the old Car-mine Gym, that is a very old school place in New York, and love The Battery Park movie theatre where it's always easy to get a seat," said Rob-ert. "We, and they, love The New Museum which is huge for the Bowery, and they marvel at The High Line. New York is really an amazing place for kids."

The New Museum, founded in 1977, is the only museum in the world that is exclusively devot-ed to contemporary art from around the world. In 2007, it moved to 235 Bowery, in the Bowery neighborhood. The building, co-designed by To-kyo architects SANAA and New York architects Gensler, is considered a global icon, and it has greatly expanded space for exhibitions.

The High Line
The panoramic win-dow in the Standard Hotel bar in the Meatpacking District that was built right over the High Line, the new city park built on a disused el-evated railway.

The High Line is an incredible place, too. It is a park created in 2009 along a railway line built in 1930, and has been trans-formed by James Corner's famous landscape archi-tecture firm Field Oper-ations, in collaboration with the Diller Scofidio +

Two original examples of **mural decoration** in the Meatpacking District.

"New York is an amazing place, but it is the people of the City which make it so unique."

Renfro studio. The long promenade runs through modern architecture, green spaces, public art, chairs and benches, fountains, flea markets, coffee places and wine bars, still showing portions of the old railway. It begins in the Meatpacking District and Chelsea Markets, surrounded by the impressive Standard Hotel and panoramic Tenth Avenue Square and Viewing Platform, with its view of the Empire State Building. Frank Gehry's IAC building, and Jean Nouvel's condo at 100 11th Street also frame the landscape.

But Cortney and Robert have contributed to the creation of other amazing spaces in the city, like Lulu's, the new nightclub inside the W Hotel in Hoboken, New Jersey, which opened for the 2014 Super Bowl. "We wanted to create a concept of new design that combines contemporary flair and vintage, as it is in our style, but also a special place, a new concept as a nightclub," says Cortney.

"What I like about it is that people that don't usually go to the Guggenheim Museum – another place I love in New York – or to a museum, can see art," points out Robert.

The food display in the **Chelsea Market**.

"New York is, and will always be, the greatest city in the world.
There is no other place that has the energy
that you can find in this place."

"Over the bar, with a glass wall overlooking Manhattan skylines, you can see Murano glass chandeliers, hand-painted columns in bright yellow and green by the British artist Richard Woods, textiles by Sarah Morris, a vintage pool table, big art works like a photo of Mick Jagger transformed into a tiger by Damien Hirst, and one of a naked Kate Moss holding a cigarette, by Mario Testino. You can also reach the W Hotel in Hoboken by ferry from Lower Manhattan, a ride that gives you a wonderful view of the skyline.

"Another place I really like outside Manhattan is Woodstock. In June 2014, we worked on the interior design of The Hotel Dylan, a boutique hotel, which has the flair of a small contemporary museum. This is, in part, because of the art work we chose and the fact that every room is different from every other, with true bohemian sophistication. It evokes film director and screenwriter Wes Anderson's style, inspired by his whimsical humor in *Moonrise Kingdom* (2012). In front of the hotel is a restaurant and music venue.

The Chelsea Market
A favorite with New Yorkers, the Chelsea Market, located in the former Nabisco biscuit factory, features delicatessens, pastry shops, cafes, restaurants and shops. And there is no lack of cultural events.

"For me, New York is first of all gray.
Here, it's all about steel,
but, most of all, we wish the future
of New York City to stay cool."

A **hot dog vendor** in the Meatpacking District.
The **Meatpacking District at night**, with artistic illumination.

"The Hotel Dylan is a music-themed homage to the big music tradition of Woodstock and its legendary concert in 1969, mixing up modern and vintage furniture. Each room has a record player with original records, Elliott Landy photographs, and iconic tie-dye flower artwork by Michael De Feo, who created a huge sculpture on one side of the hotel too," says Robert. "It is on the famous RT 28 and it is owned by the Wall Street trader and entrepreneur Paul Covello, who grew up in Woodstock, and his business partner David Mazzullo, who grew up spending family vacations in the Catskills. It is a quiet and romantic place to get away from New York City both in summer and winter, but also a place full of character," adds Cortney.

New York is a city of colors that Robert and Cortney love. "We both love colors. I love all colors, I must admit," confesses Cortney. "But what I noticed in New York is Black – from The Ramones to Lou Reed to Joan Jett. They all wore black. And they were the reasons I wanted to move to New York, as a young girl, from a small town in Georgia."

"For me, New York is first of all gray. Here, it's all about steel," adds Robert. "But, most of all, we wish the future of New York City to stay cool."

YOKO ONO

The "Memory" of the City

She is known for her work in avant-garde art, music, and filmmaking. She was the muse of John Lennon and of many other artists of her generation. And, today, she is still a world famous multimedia artist, singer and peace activist. Yoko Ono is an icon in New York history.

She remembers the original feeling she had for the City. "The first time I saw New York was when I was anywhere from 4 to 6 years old. We were living in San Francisco then, and came to see the World's Fair which was then in New York," she says. She was born in Tokyo, daughter of a father who was a banker, who came from a long line of samurai warrior-scholars, and a mother who had been a classical pianist. The kanji translation of her first name means "ocean child." Her father was transferred to San Francisco two weeks before her birth and the family followed soon after. She was enrolled in piano lessons when she was only four years old.

In 1937, they were all transferred back to Japan and she went to Gakushuin, at that time one of the most exclusive schools in Japan. But they all soon came back to America. It was in 1940 that the family moved to New York City, and the following year they had to go back to Japan again. They were even there during the great firebombing in 1945. They sheltered in a special bunker

> I just like the hustle and the bustle of the city. It gives electricity for your mind.

and, later, Yoko, with some family members, went to the Karuizawa mountain resort and were forced to beg for food, while her father ended up in a concentration camp in Asia. It was during this time that she experienced what it meant to have to fight to survive and she understood what it really meant to be an "outsider".

In 1946, she went back to the Gakushuin school, near the imperial palace, and she had Prince Akihito, the future emperor of Japan, as a classmate. After graduation, in 1951, she was accepted as the first woman to enter the philosophy department of Gakushuin University, but left after just two semesters. After the war, her family moved, without her, to Scarsdale, New York, and she rejoined them there.

She recalls how New York has changed over the years. "I remember the first hotel we stayed in was the Riverside Hotel. It was uptown, off Broadway. It doesn't exist now. That's how much it has changed. But I saw the time told, in neon, on the New Jersey side from my hotel bedroom then. So some things are not far off now," she remembers.

New York has inspired her creative process as an artist in different ways. "From the 20s to the 50s, the art world was influenced heavily by Eastern Art, not the other way around.

The romantic **Bow Bridge** in Central Park.

A view of **Central Park** in autumn.

"Everywhere and every person is interesting. Why they stay in this polluted city of mind and body, me included, is a wonder."

"There are a few books in the United States and Europe about that, written by Western critics if you wish to read them," she points out.

Even if her parents did not always approve, Yoko, when she became a student at Sarah Lawrence College, mixed with many artists and poets who had a "bohemian" lifestyle.

Taking part in art happenings and visiting many galleries, Yoko had the desire to display her own art and so she started doing it in her Chambers Street loft, in Tribeca, using it as a performance space. She liked to experiment, so much so that once she even set a painting on fire during a performance. After many personal adventures,

she became involved in New York's downtown art scene and the Fluxus group. Her circle of friends in New York included, among many others, Dan Richter, Jonas Mekas, Merce Cunningham, Fred DeAsis, Peggy Guggenheim, Keith Haring, and Andy Warhol.

Today, she still has a very distinctive feeling for New York. "I just like the hustle and the bustle of the city. It gives electricity for your mind," she confesses, while she thinks of her favorite places here, without naming any of them. "Everywhere and every person is interesting. Why they stay in this polluted city of mind and body, me included, is a wonder," she reflects.

"I am always looking for a chance to communicate an idea that will make the world better. I thought making a peace garden in which trees and pebbles of all different countries exist together would say something. And, IMAGINE CIRCLE!"

Her New York is very special and magical, as if it had been painted by a master painter in the mind of the artist she is. Her colors for the City? "Charcoal grey buildings and strikingly beautiful blue sky," she thinks. If she had to think of some music for New York, what would it be? "DOG-TOWN, composed by me."

Yoko Ono met John Lennon for the first time in 1966, while she was doing her own art exhibition in London and while he was still part of The Beatles. Officially, they became a couple in 1968 and worked together on projects. They even used their honeymoon as a stage for public protests against the Vietnam War, and for peace. Their 1969 "Bed-Ins for Peace" in Amsterdam and Montreal are famous. Yoko also had a big influence on Lennon's music. With him she co-wrote, among other songs, *Give Peace a Chance* and the experimental *Revolution #9* and they worked on many other projects together. New York had a big influence on their artistic inspiration and production. After the Beatles disbanded Yoko and Lennon lived together in London and then in New York.

And so she remembers a time of love, when she arrived here with John Lennon.

Dakota Building
This is the building overlooking Central Park where Yoko Ono lived with John Lennon (she still lives there).

Imagine Circle

The mosaic with the title of John Lennon's famous song is at the Strawberry Fields Memorial in Central Park, which Yoko Ono dedicated to her husband.

"Love, love, love from one who is still
in love with Planet Earth."

"We would never have been allowed to come back in because of the immigration problem we were having with the United States government at the time. We wanted to clear our names so we could come back in. Both John and I loved the city, but if we didn't have that, we might have come and gone," she recalls, referring to their deep "need" to be here.

Looking for a place to live they decided on the beautiful Dakota Building on Central Park West, overlooking the park. "Jack Palance, who was in the film I was making then, called *IMAGINE*, told me about the Dakota – that I should check it because John and I would like it. He was right," she remembers.

Like many artists, they both had quite a turbulent life, but even if separated, they were always close, until John Lennon was shot dead in front of the Dakota Building in December 1980 by Mark David Chapman, a deranged fan who had been stalking him for months. They had been working in a studio on *Walking on Thin Ice (For John)*, and John wanted to go back, before dinner, to see his son before he was put to bed. The single was released less than a month later.

After Lennon's death Yoko received commercial success as part of the Plastic Ono Band and for her art and music work. Recognition of her art came from the Whitney Museum exhibition in 1989 and from many retrospectives of her work, like the one in the Japan Society in New York City in 2001 and others around the world.

Since Lennon's death Ono has been working to preserve his legacy. She funded, and she is maintaining, Strawberry Fields in New York City and the Imagine Peace Tower in Iceland. And she is always active as a philanthropist for the arts and for peace, all over the world.

Fabulous Scenery
When there is heavy snowfall in New York, Central Park becomes an enchanting 'Scandinavian' landscape for New Yorkers and tourists.

Imagine Peace by Yoko Ono in **Times Square**.

She has a daughter from her marriage to Anthony Cox, a jazz musician, film producer and art promoter, and she had a son with John Lennon, Sean Taro Ono Lennon, who is also a musician.

Regarding the Strawberry Fields Memorial in remembrance of Lennon, she just followed her heart, her passion and her love, as she has always done. "I am always looking for a chance to communicate an idea that will make the world better. I thought making a peace garden in which trees and pebbles of all different countries exist together would say something. And, IMAGINE CIRCLE! You don't know how much resistance I got from people in power to create that one," she says.

Strawberry Fields, a triangular section of Central Park just opposite the Dakota Building, is named after John Lennon's song *Strawberry Fields Forever*. It was designed by Bruce Kelly, the chief landscape architect for the Central Park Conservancy, and was dedicated by Yoko Ono and New York Mayor Ed Koch, on what would have been Lennon's 45th birthday, October 9, 1985. Its entrance is on West 72nd Street and Central Park West and its focal point is a circular pathway mosaic of inlaid stones, with, in the center, the word "Imagine". It is often covered with flowers, candles and other objects by Lennon's fans and by tourists. On Lennon's birthday, and on the anniversary of his death, people gather to sing songs and pay tribute.

Imagine Peace
Part of Yoko Ono's multimedia project shown on luminous billboards in Times Square on the occasion of International Peace Day on September 21st.

IMAGINE PEACE

love, yoko

IMAGINE PEACE

love, yoko

GEORGE
· M ·
COHAN

1878-1942

The **MoMA** Sculpture Garden and the entrance hall.

"New York Artists are super intelligent, cool and funky. We are already one step ahead as well, creating a Brave New World."

Nowadays, Yoko is still a very active artist. And one of her most beloved pieces in New York is the *Wish Tree* (1981-present), in which a tree, native to the installation site, is installed. "Make a wish/ Write it down on a piece of paper/ Fold it and tie it around a branch of a Wish Tree/ Ask your friends to do the same/ Keep wishing/ Until the branches are covered with wishes," say the instructions on her 1996 Wish Piece. Her Wish Tree Installation is in the Sculpture Garden of the Museum of Modern Art, established in 2010, and has had contributions from all over the world. At the same time, in 2014, Yoko, after several successful albums, released *Angel*, which went to the top of the US Dance chart.

As an artist, how does she see New York developing in the future? "New York Artists are super intelligent, cool and funky. We are already one step ahead as well, creating a Brave New World – as Aldous and Laura Huxley imagined it will be and it is," she explains. What does she wish for? "Love, love, love from one who is still in love with Planet Earth. Yoko."

The MoMA
The Museum of Modern Art building was designed by the Japanese architect Yoshio Taniguchi. In the museum garden is the *Wish Tree*, an installation created by Yoko Ono.

The Mus

AL PACINO

The "Legend" of the City

His name is a legend all over the world. Al Pacino is one of the most incredibly talented and compelling actors in the history of cinema. His expressions, his way of talking, his way of improvising, the acting which he expresses in the physicality of the body, as if it were his own language, create a magic spell, capable of gripping you even more than the thousands lights of the city. Al Pacino, who also moved to Los Angeles because of his work, while still keeping an apartment in Manhattan, is a real New Yorker. And he is one of those personalities who admits to having the city in his blood and in his soul, even when he is far away, like the memory of his childhood, while he was growing up and becoming the celebrity he is today. And he still remembers New York how it used to be. Rough, beautiful, and real.

> I have my own method of acting... My thing is coming to the words eventually, making the words part of me. In that sense I am really unpredictable, just like New York is.

"I was born in Manhattan and I was raised in East Harlem in my early years," he remembers. "When my parents split after the war, my father was in the army and then a salesman, my mother and I moved in with her parents in the South Bronx: my grandfather was an immigrant from Corleone, Sicily. We were all living together in a three-room apartment. I had one of the greatest relationships of my life with my grandfather."

His love for acting existed from the beginning.

"I grew up as an only child and I had a great imagination. I was always having fun, building and creating stories. It helped to fill up my loneliness," he says. "But storytelling ran in the family. When the weather was good, my grandfather and I sat on the roof of our tenement building and he told me tales about his rough youth in New York. He just loved talking to me and I loved to listen."

Al Pacino even had a very special way to discover the city around him. "At the same time I was listening to my grandfather's stories, I was listening to New York, from the roof. There were all these voices and sounds coming up from the streets. There were the Poles, the Italians, the Jews, the Germans, the Irish, and the Latinos. This incredible melting pot is where I came from. I have always thought that it was like some Eugene O'Neill play. That was New York for me then. Now that I haven't taken the subway or eaten in a deli for years, as I have to deal with the fame of having become what I am now, I sometimes miss that, but I know that it is and will always be inside me."

All his memories of the place he grew up and became famous in, are still there, alive in his heart, like it was yesterday. And through his words, you can discover an old New York, which barely exists today.

Billboards, taxi and neon signs in **Times Square**.

"Other things I liked to do in New York, when I was a kid, were jumping between the roofs of tenement buildings. I wasn't allowed out and it was rough, but it was a lot of fun. There is a whole life up on the roofs in New York. Another one of my favorite places was called "the Dutchies," a swampy labyrinth on the Bronx River, where kids used to hide in the high marsh grasses."

Even if acting was already pulsing in him like the fire of knowledge, he was initiated into the theater by his mother. "My mother, Rose, had a special connection to the theater, which she gave to me too. She took me to see Tennessee Williams' *Cat on a Hot Tin Roof* on Broadway once, a play that I loved and which inspired me so much. But to support us she had many jobs, she worked as a cinema usherette too. So, when I was three years old, she began to take me to the movies. Sometimes my mother even took me to the movies when she came home from work and that became our kind of date. And the next day I would act out all the parts! I think that is how I started. At the beginning I was just performing in front of my extended family," he explains.

The street life of New York, which is still a big element of the city today, was a special part of his life in the times when he was growing up here. "In New York, in the Forties and Fifties, people escaped their small apartments to hang out on the streets, under street lamps, to roll dice or

Celebrating the New Year
Since 1907 a New Year's Ball has been raised to the top of a pole on the One Times Square Building and then lowered, to mark the arrival of the new year before a huge crowd.

Vintage buildings near Washington Square Park.

play poker or just to meet and talk. But instead, I was performing or asking others to perform with me, to make friends," he says about his way of adapting to street life.

"The characters I met on the New York streets then, particularly from gangs or wherever, I modelled many of my memorable characters on. I had the best time of my life, and that had also been a great start and inspiration for my profession."

He was very connected to his teachers, who recognized his talent immediately. "I also went into the drama world at school, where I had a wonderful teacher. I love teachers, as some of them were my mentors. One of them came to my grandmother, to our apartment, and sat down with her to convince her that she should encourage me to act, as we were not rich, and being an actor was a kind of exotic profession for my family," he confesses.

It was certainly not easy to make it, but the striving to make it in theater and perform was stronger than everything else. And at that time New York had a special flair and offered young actors a kind of "school of life" in acting. "I was fascinated by the experimental Living Theater in the early 1960s and by the Open Theater.

Washington Square Park
During a rainstorm the greenery is magical in Washington Square Park, which is surrounded by one of the loveliest zones in Greenwich Village.

> "The characters I met on the New York streets then, particularly from gangs or wherever, I modelled many of my memorable characters on. I had the best time of my life, and that had also been a great start and inspiration for my profession."

"The café-theater era impressed me, when you could go to a coffeehouse, anywhere in The Village, and see wonderful pieces being played by actors for the price of a cappuccino or a pastry. After the performance, they passed hats around to collect money for their meal that day. I became one of them. I used to perform in coffee houses, up to 60 performances a week, to make a living like that," he says.

But even then, he was already different, he was distinguishing himself from all the others with his special talent and he was developing those unique characters, which will always be in the history of cinema and of humanity itself. "I have my own method of acting. I don't believe in memorizing lines. That's not how I prepare a role. My thing is coming to the words eventually, making the words part of me. In that sense I am really unpredictable, just like New York is," he points out.

And in his eyes, as in his enchanting smile, you recognize, from time to time, some of the iconic roles he played in the city. He is a method actor, taught mainly by Lee Strasberg and Charles Laughton at the Actors Studio in New York. But in every character he puts something of himself, making it unforgettable and unique in his performance, or it is just his ability to make it believable.

Can we forget him in *Dog Day Afternoon* (1975), shot almost entirely on a quiet stretch of Prospect Park West between 17th and 18th Street, in Brooklyn? Or as Michael Corleone in *The Godfather* (1972) and its sequels *The Godfather Part II* (1974) and *The Godfather Part III* (1990), the epic saga about the mafia and gangsters in America, and as an incorruptible cop in *Serpico* (1973), a film about Frank Serpico, a real-life New York police officer who was betrayed by his fellow officers when he uncovered illegal activity within the department? Or in *Carlito's Way* (1993), shot mostly in Spanish Harlem, or *Scent of a Woman* (1992), for which he won an Academy Award for Best Actor? Even today, walking inside The Waldorf Astoria, one of the historical New York hotels, one's imagination drifts to one of the most memorable scenes from *Scent of a Woman* – when Al Pacino dances the tango with a much younger woman in The Vanderbilt Room. There are these unforgettable moments that are part of his unending contribution to the story of his New York, which he keeps on bringing to life every time he performs, nearly every year, on the stage of Broadway. Because Al does not simply speak the lines, he feels them, communicating an emotional authenticity which only a great artist is able to achieve and which he says he discovers every time and in every unpredictable moment of living in New York.

The MetLife Building seen from the **Waldorf Astoria Hotel** along Park Avenue.

CATHLEEN SCHINE
The "Doglover" of the City

Cathleen Schine is a best-selling author, one of New York's most popular and best-loved. Her New York is not the City of fashionable blocks. It is not the City of mansions, narrow houses of historical importance, or of glamour. It is the City of brownstones that line the streets which were broken up into apartments that are now mostly rentals and rent-controlled. It is the City that, in this way, has partly escaped the sweep of gentrification, a place where struggling musicians, actors, secretaries and window washers can still afford to live, some of them growing successful, some simply growing old. Here, commercial ventures still exist side by side with a street's residents. And it is a place where a street's proximity to Central Park makes it a favorite with professional dog walkers and dog owners. This is the New York of her novel *The New Yorkers*, a book in which dogs are some of the main characters.

"*The New Yorkers* is a kind of love letter to New York City. It is about the New York that I know, which has neighborhoods and seasons, and the rhythms, sometimes, of a small town. The novel is about falling in love, neighbors falling in and out of love, all of this happening on one block. And then, there are the dogs, who are New Yorkers too: a dignified old white pit-bull named Be-atrice, a puppy named Howdy discovered in the closet of a dead man, a boisterous Rottweiler named Kaiya, and of course poor Jolly, a vicious little mutt. In the magical way of New York City, dogs bring people together, and I wanted to show that in the book. The dogs in *The New Yorkers* act as cupids. I also created a corner restaurant called the Go Go Grill whose owners allow you to bring in your dogs. That was wishful thinking. In fact, city sanitation laws strictly forbid dogs in restaurants and hand out hefty tickets. But it has always been a fantasy of mine, this kind of restaurant, so why not make it happen in the one place I can, in a book?" This block is on the Upper West Side, somewhere just around the corner from Nora Ephron territory and a Woody Allen movie. In her 2004 *New Yorker* essay *Dog Trouble*, Schine had already talked about a very special dog named Buster, an adorable, helplessly mad mutt she rescued. As Buster gradually revealed his dangerously violent, as well as self-destructive, temperament, he alienated Schine's friends and family as well as other dog owners on the Upper West Side, driving her in desperation to a series of dog trainers, dog shrinks, dog chiropractors and even a dog acupuncturist... until she herself was rescued by the joy of a cairn terrier puppy named Hector.

> New York, for me, is home.
> New York is reality, normality.
> Every other place feels like a vacation or exile.

"People don't realize what a good place New York is for dogs. New York is stimulating for human beings, and it's stimulating for dogs."

Both Buster and Hector allowed Schine to discover the New York of dogs and their owners and inspired her to write *The New Yorkers*, which is about the unique relationship between city-dwellers and their dogs. The friendly nature of dogs, and their need to be walked, forces their masters, even the most reclusive ones, into social situations. The dogs in New York bark at one another, sniff one another, inspect each other's most intimate body parts; they lick the hands of strangers and jump up at passersby who cannot resist them and their affectionate nature. They create moments of intimacy in the lives of people who may have lived side by side for years without ever speaking to one another. Dogs in New York bring people together, even shy, monastic people. Dogs are as much New Yorkers as the people who walk them, for they genuinely enjoy the city and create a community for their owners.

The New Yorkers
Dogs playing in the snow in Central Park. Just as occurs in Cathleen Schine's novel, in a megalopolis like New York, taking a walk with your dog is an occasion for socializing.

Central Park and Dogs
Even in winter and when it is snowing one can come across inhabitants of Manhattan walking with their dogs on the snow-clad roads of Central Park. Dogs are also citizens of New York City.

A **dog sitter** taking a group of dogs along a road in Central Park.

They feel at home, and they let their owners feel at home with them.

"As a child in Connecticut I dreamed of growing up to become a graduate student. My mother was a graduate student for so long that I thought it was an occupation. Years later, my ambitions were realized when I entered the University of Chicago's graduate program in medieval history. Unfortunately, once there, I noticed I had no memory for names, dates or abstract ideas. Sadly, I had to abandon that dream, but, after a period in Italy on a fellowship studying paleography, I found out I like shoes," she recalls. "So I pursued a career in this area, which was rewarding, but short-lived, as I could not get a job. In debt and increasingly desperate, I turned to the lucrative career of free-lance writing, in which I remained in debt and desperate until I began to write novels. That's what I always wanted to do but never had the courage to until there was no place else to turn." Schine has written for *The New Yorker*, is a regular contributor to *The New York Review of Books* and has written nine novels, among them *The Love Letter*, *Rameau's Niece*, *The New Yorkers*, *The Three Weissmanns of Westport*, and, most recently, *Fin & Lady*.

"Most of my books are set, at least partly, in New York. I grew up about an hour outside of the city,

but we had friends who lived here whom we would visit. They lived in a duplex penthouse on Central Park West with a view of the Museum of Natural History and Central Park. As a child, therefore, I thought all New Yorkers lived in a duplex penthouse on Central Park West with a view of the Museum of Natural History and Central Park. Naturally, I thought it was the most glamorous place in the world. And I was right," she remembers.

"I have always loved Central Park, but as I've gotten older I have come to need Central Park more and more. The things that brought me to New York in my twenties – the energy and excitement of the city – now sometimes feel like simply frenetic noise. But all I have to do is step into the park and I can feel the grandness of the city in a peaceful, quiet way. Grand Central Station is another favorite place. I've been looking up at that dark blue ceiling, with the gold constellations, my whole life. It's like a cathedral. I love the subway, too. I don't always love it when I'm in it, but I love that it exists – it's miraculous to live in a city in which you really, really don't need a car – at all. Ever," she says, thinking of her favorite places in the City.

"I lived on the Upper West Side for many years and spent a lot of happy hours walking the dog in Central Park.

The Loeb Boathouse restaurant in Central Park overlooks the lake.

"When I think of the color of New York, this may seem odd, it's green. Perhaps that's because I have spent so much time in the park over the last decade or so."

"I think Central Park on the west side in the seventies is one of the most beautiful places in the world. And the Loeb Boathouse, overlooking the river at sunset, that's a lovely New York experience. We now have an apartment on the Upper East Side in a neighborhood called Carnegie Hill. It's very quiet and elegant and everything closes early – not like the West Side at all – but I still love it. It has a really good bookstore, The Corner Bookstore, it's close to so many museums, and we're right on the park."

And which places does Hector, her doggie, like? "He is happy everywhere in New York. People don't realize what a good place New York is for dogs.

"New York is stimulating for human beings, and it's stimulating for dogs. There are so many things to smell – for dogs; the smells are not always as interesting for humans, I admit – so much information – and so many other dogs. So Hector is quite content in the city – exhausted and content. Just like me," she says. "Having a dog in New York made me fall in love with the City all over again.

"Most people in New York really live not in the whole City but in their own neighborhood, and by having a dog who has to be taken out and walked three or four times a day, I got to know my neigh-borhood in a much more intimate way than I ever had before. And I met all my neighbors, because they were out walking their dogs. I heard all the gossip and learned about everyone's children and illnesses – New York City turned into a small vil-lage. I also saw things I never noticed before – architectural details, trees, the way the light hits certain buildings at certain times. Having a dog both expanded my experience of the City and made the City smaller in scale, more accessible," she reflects. "Dogs in New York are better social-ized than dogs in most places. They have to be. And I wonder if you can see a more diverse pop-ulation of dogs anywhere."

New York never stops inspiring Cathleen, as you can see in her novels."It's funny how, now that I'm in California, so much of my imagina-tion resides completely in New York. Most of my books take place almost entirely in New York. Nostalgia? Habit? Loyalty? New York is reality for me. What happens in New York matters to me, so, I suppose, what matters in my books often ends up happening in New York," she says. *Fin & Lady* is an-other New York love letter, a discovery of a different neighborhood and time.

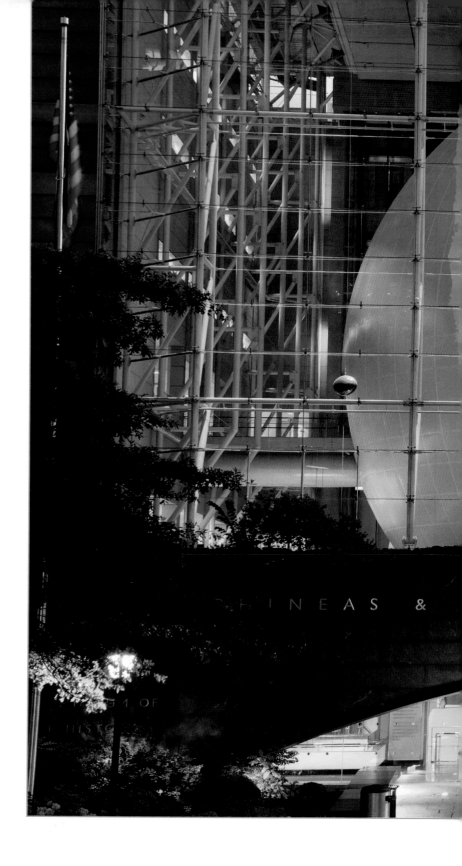

The Hayden Planetarium
One of the major attractions in the Upper West Side, the Rose Center for Earth and Space is part of the American Museum of Natural History.

"I lived on the Upper West Side for many years and spent
a lot of happy hours walking the dog in Central Park."

Brownstone buildings in the **Upper West Side**.

It is a bittersweet elegy of Greenwich Village in the 1960s, about an 11-year-old boy after the death of his parents, who is left in the not-so-reliable hands of his 24-year-old free-spirited, half-sister, Lady. She believes that the best way to raise him, in 1964, is not in the elegant uptown apartment she has inherited from her mother, but in a crazy and artistic world, full of rock-and-roll and blues and folk music – Greenwich Village. In the days of the civil rights movement and the anti war movement, Lady and Fin move into a half-finished and half-furnished townhouse on Charles Street, and into the thick of political and social upheaval.

"New York, for me, is home. New York is reality, normality. Every other place feels like a vacation or exile," she says. "When I think of the color of New York, this may seem odd, it's green. Perhaps that's because I have spent so much time in the park over the last decade or so. I think before that I would have said gray," she said.

"But there is another important New York color. In spring, there is a moment, the first day the sun really shines after the long dark winter, when the sky is deep bright blue and all the taxicabs suddenly take on a rich yellow color that I have never seen anywhere else. An exclusively New York color: Springtime taxi-cab yellow!"

Historic Buildings

In parts of the Upper West Side the brick buildings and fire escape ladders on the facades take us back to the New York City of the past.

MARTIN SCORSESE
The "Heart" of the City

Sweet and sour, light and dark, high and low; the sparkling and the obscure sides of the metropolitan soul: life on the edge. In his movies, New York pumps vividly, like blood, through the body, awakening the senses as scenes change unexpectedly, unpredictably, in fractal movements of intense emotion: passion and love, joy and anger, good and evil, life and death. And, while seeing all the faces of New York, including its darkness, we are taken back through history, to its origins, where everything began.

"For me New York is not the sparkling city of a thousand lights, but street life New York, with its crime, its contradictions, and its dark side. I have grown up knowing that kind of atmosphere, and so it is the New York I know – the one that you don't see immediately on the superficial side, but that you have to dig deeper to get to know it," he reflects.

Martin Scorsese, with his intense passion and humanity, is the "Heart" of the City, and you feel its rhythm beating in the life of his art. "New York is a subtle realism that can make you dream and think at the same time. And, above all, it can make you feel," he says. This is his gift – to be a magician, who casts his spell through the people he directs, creating photographic fragments of life and history that remain unforgettably imprinted in the memory.

> New York is a City where you always have the feeling that at any moment you can take one chance and miss another one.

To him, "New York is unique and special. I appreciate it even more when I travel a lot and then come back. It is a very exciting place, where you can identify yourself with the City itself. New Yorkers walk on the street and mix with each other as if all part of the same community," Scorsese says. "But what makes New York different from every other city in the world is its great energy and its people, different ethnic groups that live together. Sometimes we undervalue New York; we complain too much, we don't realize how lucky we are to live here."

In all of Scorsese's movies of the City, we instantly recognize that special touch of flair that has made him one of the greatest directors of all time. Certain scenes evoke early Federico Fellini, Michelangelo Antonioni, or Roberto Rossellini. "They all inspired me," he says. Because, for him, it's all about the characters, it's all about the people, as it was for these amazing masters of the cinema.

"As a director it is hard and wonderful at the same time," he points out. Referring to the making of *The Wolf of Wall Street* (2013), his film based on Jordan Belfort's memoir of the same name about the world of New York bankers and Wall Street, Scorsese's remark also echoes the New York economy and business spirit, the era of traders, financiers and the environment of bank-

> "It is very important to remember your roots
> and where you come from, to remember your culture,
> the tradition and not only the progress."

ing that comprises Lower Manhattan. "New York is a City where you always have the feeling that at any moment you can take one chance and miss another one," he observes.

Fiction and reality blend in Scorsese's productions, becoming "real" in their own way. To him, "New York is like a mirror, where the image is perfect, until the mirror breaks and each fragment continues to reflect it, but now from different angles. It is broken, and painful to look at, but for that imperfection, it becomes more beautiful. And somehow, it still works." So, you can discover New York in the gleam of a skyscraper, in the back window of a taxi, or lights that clear suddenly in the water of a pond. We see it in a silhouette reflected on an eye, the fearless courage of a gangster, and the proud heart of a woman ready to fight for love or simply to let it go. The City is revealed in a surreal moment, in a man who looks behind a glass full of raindrops. That simple touch of humanity can be recognized, every time. And often that humanity is Italian. "When I was a boy I lived in a neighborhood where they were mostly Sicilian or from Sicilian heritage," he remembers. Martin Scorsese was born and raised in New York. His father, Charles (1913-1993) and his mother, Catherine (1912-1997), both worked in Manhattan's Garment District.

Although Charles worked as a clothes presser and Catherine as a seamstress, both parents were also actors. "This art has always been in my genes," he says.

Martin Scorsese's House
The building where the famous director grew up is in the Nolita neighborhood north of Little Italy.

Garment District
The Garment District in 1948: 35th Street jammed with trucks. Scorsese's parents worked in the city's 'fashion quarter.'

The **Needle Threading a Button** in Garment District.

"New York is a subtle realism that can make you dream and think at the same time."

Their roots were in Polizzi Generosa, a small village in the province of Palermo, Sicily, where his grandparents came from. The whole family moved to Little Italy before Martin started school, and he grew up as a Roman Catholic, although he still feels he is, above everything, an American. "I have Italian heritage, but I know that I am an American and, first of all, a New Yorker," he declares. "It is very important to remember your roots and where you come from, to remember your culture, the tradition and not only the progress."

How did Scorsese start loving movies? "I was fascinated by the cinema world since I was four or five years old.

"I love the colors, the images, I was watching these figures of people moving and telling stories which inspired my fantasy. And I was also rediscovering New York in many movies I

The Garment Worker
Detail of the sculpture executed by the Israeli artist Judith Weller as a tribute to the workers in the fashion-oriented Garment District.

Life on **Prince Street** in the SoHo area.
Detail of the facade of a historic building in **SoHo**.

"New York is unique and special. I appreciate it even more when I travel a lot and then come back."

watched, where it was featured. But I already had my own New York in mind, which is the one you see in my movies," he recalls.

"I had asthma as a boy, and I could not play sports or be out in the street like other kids, so my parents or my older brother would often take me to movie theaters. I knew the street life, but at the same time, I was living in my imaginary world, like Hugo, the child character in my film of the same name, *Hugo* (2011). Hugo lives alone in the Gare Montparnasse railway station in Paris. For him it was that world, while for me it was New York and the world of the City."

As he developed a passion for cinema, Scors-

ese's connection with New York grew with the same intensity. "When I was eleven years old, I started going by myself to a cinema only a few blocks away down the street," he recalls, "I know what it means to be lonely or isolated. Just as the boy, Hugo, hid in a big clock, I did the same in a New York church. I was sitting in an empty church, in the silence, and it was as if I meditated. I isolated myself from everything – from the crowded two and three bedroom apartments, from the noise of the streets, where people would shout or fight, from the chaos of the traffic and of the City."

"But life on the street doesn't just have negative sides. It helps to relate to others, to find friends,

and also to understand how important it is to have a family. Family is, for sure, one of the most important values in life," he adds.

The filmmaker was fascinated by Italian Neorealism since he was a boy – movies like *The Bicycle Thief* (1948), *Paisà* (1946), *Rome, Open City* (1945) – and would later direct the documentary *Il Mio Viaggio in Italia (My Voyage to Italy)* (2001), in which he narrates his journey through Italian cinema. He adored French New Wave cinema and directors like Robert Bresson, and was inspired by other great directors, like Ingmar Bergman. "Their images were also a way of rediscovering New York," he explains.

All of Scorsese's education was in the City. He graduated from Cardinal Hayes High School in the Bronx and attended what is now known as the College of Arts and Sciences, followed by the Tisch School of the Arts, New York University's film school, places that will be in his memory forever. He explored his ethnic roots with the documentary *ITALIANAMERICAN* (1974), in which he featured his parents, while he developed his own New York with such masterpieces as *Mean Streets* (1973), *Taxi Driver* (1976), *New York, New York* (1977), *Raging Bull* (1980), and *Goodfellas* (1990), all starring Robert De Niro. The actor and Scorsese are now lifelong friends as well as collaborators, both being New York "souls".

Italian-American Pride
The inhabitants of Little Italy are very proud of their origins, as can be seen during street fairs.

After Hours (1985), filmed in SoHo, about one increasingly unfortunate night for a mild-mannered New York word processor, has become a cult film and offers an iconic portrait

of the City. *The Age of Innocence* (1993), a period adaptation of Edith Wharton's novel of the same name, is a portrait of high society in late 19th-century New York. It shows a historical moment in the City, and was partly shot at one of the most beautiful locations, Gramercy Park.

In *Gangs of New York* (2002), Scorsese showed the endemic violence rampant in the sub-cultural and ethnic divisions that made the City. "The gangs are connected to the roots and the creation of the City itself, and they were part of that criminal street life to which I feel connected and drawn to analyze," he says.

The film was shot in New Jersey and Long Island, as well as New York. "New York is an open air set, but because of the high costs, I've also been shooting a lot out of the City. For *The Departed* (2006), for instance, we had to shoot some scenes in Red Hook, Brooklyn, but I hope we can go back to shooting more and more again in the streets of New York," he explains.

In 1990, Scorsese set up The Film Foundation, a non-profit organization dedicated to film preservation, and in 2007 he created The World Cinema Foundation.

Restaurants in Little Italy

The restaurants and cafés with their tables on the sidewalks make this neighborhood even more lively and charming.

Italian Roots

An Italian bakery on Prince Street, in the heart of SoHo. Scorsese's Italian origin has had an influence on his film-making.

"New Yorkers walk on the street and mix with each other as if all part of the same community.
But what makes New York different from every other city in the world is its great energy and its people, different ethnic groups that live together."

5th Avenue
One of the most famous thoroughfares in Manhattan, 5th Avenue begins at the Washington Square Arch, passes through Midtown and ends in Harlem.

Washington Square Park
The large park in Greenwich Village is a favorite among New Yorkers. Some scenes in famous films set in the city were shot here.

For him, "cinema is part of the story of humanity itself." In the same way, he loves and portrays New York like a wonderful example of human society.

In his movies, New York contains his Italian-American identity and Catholic heritage, including its guilt and redemption, its conflicts and weaknesses, like gang violence and modern crime and profanity. And now, since he became a father again, there is also a certain romanticism in the filmmaker: "I have been very lucky. I had children in my twenties and then when I was fifty-seven years old. When I was older, I had more experience and patience," he confides. "Now I spend a lot of time with my youngest daughter and think she has influenced my way of seeing things."

Regarding New York, Martin Scorsese continues to be fascinated by the stories of the City: "I still go where the story takes me in the City. I'm still following the sound and beat of New York."

TAYLOR SWIFT
The "Ambassador" of the City

When she was a child, she had a dream. She dreamt about playing with music and words. And, maybe, she also dreamt about coming to New York at some point. Nowadays, she is a star.

She is a songwriter, a writer, a singer and an actress, as we have seen in *The Giver* (2014); she is certainly one of the world's most loved and popular celebrities. Taylor Swift was born in Pennsylvania, but moved to Nashville, Tennessee at 14 to pursue a career in country music, and she soon became famous, with albums like *Taylor Swift, Fearless, Speak Now,* and *Red.* Even if she has always been coming and going from and to New York, she decided to relocate here in 2014, and her move was immediately successful.

So successful, in fact, that she has collaborated with NYC & Company as its Global Welcome Ambassador for Tourism in 2014 and 2015. It has been an international campaign to attract visitors to New York, from all over the world. "I'm still learning, but I'm so enthusiastic about this city that when I love something, I'm very vocal about it," Swift said of the title. "New York was a huge landscape for what became an album. It's affected my life in ways that I'm not even fully aware of. It's like an electric city, and I approached moving

What makes New York City New York City is that it is unlike anywhere else in the world. It's almost as if the City has its own heartbeat.

there with such wide-eyed optimism. I saw New York as a place of endless potential and possibility, and you can hear that reflected in this music and in this song."

Taylor, so young, beautiful, talented and joyful, represents every new New Yorker who comes into the City and falls in love with it or makes it his/her home, with a strong sense of optimism. And, certainly, with a great positive energy. Her heart is definitely in New York, so much so that the first song on Taylor Swift's album *1989* (the year of her birth) is called *Welcome to New York.* "Walking through a crowd, / The village is aglow / Kaleidoscope of loud / Heartbeats under coats. / Everybody here wanted something more / Searching for a sound we hadn't heard before / And it said / Welcome to New York / It's been waiting for you ..." she writes in her song. And again: "It's a new soundtrack / I could dance to this beat, beat / Forevermore / The lights are so bright / But they never blind me, me ..." Then even more: "When we first dropped our bags on apartment floors / Took our broken hearts, / Put them in a drawer / Everybody here was someone else before / And you can want who you want / Boys and boys and girls and girls...."

But Taylor is even more enthusiastic about New York,

> "You can find fashion that inspires you,
> art that inspires you, humanity that inspires you.
> Everywhere you look it's impossible not to fall
> in love or be affected by something in New York City."

Buildings in SoHo
Fire escape ladders and decorative architectural elements on a building in SoHo, the district famous for its wonderful lofts.

Architecural Details
In the past many artists lived in SoHo or had their ateliers there, which contributed to the creation of these marvelous architectural elements.

as she revealed in different videos regarding the New York City Tourism campaign. "What makes New York City New York City is that it is unlike anywhere else in the world. It's almost as if the City has its own heartbeat. You can find fashion that inspires you, art that inspires you, humanity that inspires you. Everywhere you look it's impossible not to fall in love or be affected by something in New York City," Swift says in the video. "I think what brought me to New York is still a little bit of a mystery to me. Every day I wake up with this feeling, like, 'I need to be in New York.' New York, kind of, pulled me here like a magnet. I was intimidated by the fact that it was bright and bold, and loud. And now, I know I should run toward things like that. I should run toward things that are absolutely, overwhelmingly electric. There's so much happening right in front of you, so many stories playing out, that, for my writing, it definitely helped inspire an album that is, by far, the one I am most proud of in my career," she says, talking about her feelings about New York.

Swift, who lives in the neighborhood of Tribeca,

A musical instrument store in SoHo.

then goes on describing some of the things she loves most about the city, like walking through various neighborhoods, getting a good cup of coffee or a latte, or being amazed by the vibrant energy of it. "You, kind of, remember old New York. People, kind of, picked their favorite little neighborhoods, they got to know people around their neighborhoods, they had their favorite restaurant, their favorite bar, their favorite coffee place. There are a lot of things in New York that make me really very happy. Having a good cup of coffee or a real latte is really important to me, no place does it better than New York," she realizes. "I really like that you don't really have to make a plan. If you want, you just make the day happen. Sometimes, what I like to do is pick a neighborhood and not necessarily pick a destination in the neighborhood. Today, I just think I want to walk around the West Village. Or, you know, I want to walk around the Lower East Side. And you just find places, these little, kind of, secret treasure places that you love and the day, kind of, happens in New York."

Taylor has a very clear idea about New Yorkers, like she has become, the same way that most people living in New York come from somewhere else. "People talk about Southern hospitality, and that's a real thing, but there's also a really interesting hospitality about New York too," she states in another video.

Old and New
The reflection of a building, with the characteristic cast-iron fire escape ladders, on the shop window of a SoHo design shop.

> "I saw New York as a place of endless potential and possibility."

"Yeah, people here are honest but they're also very friendly and there's also a lot of heart here. And it's easy to get around. People will help you, if you ask for help, trust me I've done it. For me, it was always this big, intimidating thing. There's a coziness to it here."

Being such a creative artist and writer, she also has her special, and magic, "New York City vocabulary" words, as she highlights in a video.

"A bodega is a corner store that's open pretty much 24 hours, most of the time. You can get almost anything in a bodega. Bodegas are our friends," she explains. "Most commonly confused with the pronunciation hugh-ten street.

Street Art
A work painted between East Houston Street and the Bowery by the Brazilian twins known as Os Gemeos, specialized in urban graffiti.

This **Bowery mural** was clearly inspired by Pop Art.

"When you get here and you see the sign, you'll think 'oh, Houston, Texas' – incorrect. Houston Street," she goes on. "And you hear people refer to NoHo or SoHo. NoHo stands for North of Houston. SoHo stands for South of Houston," she recalls. "In the South and pretty much anywhere else, the part of your house that is in front of your door and your stairs is, a lot of the time, called a porch; not in New York. Anything that's basically a stairway entry to a dwelling, home, apartment, brown-stone, or townhouse is referred to as a stoop," she points out.

Taylor Swift's New York is the New York of the "new eyes" of those who arrive here to see the lights, the architecture, the neighborhoods, and the hundreds of people on the sidewalks for the first time. They can be a tourist, they can be an im-migrant, they can be somebody who just wants to relocate with the dream of starting a new life or a new adventure, to get a new chance, to make it or to pursue its heart. But, all of this is also New York. A place where you feel at home after only a few days of being here. And, as Taylor points out, a place that, even if a big city, can become your per-sonal place, a place to be inspired, and a place to be transformed. The challenge is to find your own dimension in it, to discover your own New York. And, once you do, once you fall in love with the city, you will never get rid of it.

The Colors of the City
Graffiti and murals are two of the genres that intermingle to produce the distinc-tive New York street art.

Author

Alessandra Mattanza, author, screenwriter and fine-art photographer, was born in Italy but has lived abroad for more than twenty years.

She spent her youth in Australia and returns there regularly for professional and personal reasons. She worked as an editor for the publisher Handelsblatt in Munich. Now for several years she has been living in New York and has effectively become a native of that city. In the last two years she has divided her time between New York and Los Angeles. Her infinite passion for the cinema has led her to specialize in interviews with actors and directors, as well as in traveling and fiction. She currently works as a foreign correspondent, contributor and editor for a number of publishers in Italy and Ger-many, including Rizzoli, Hearst, Mondadori, Sperling & Kupfer, Condé Nast, Cairo Editore, White Star/National Geographic/De Agostini, and Giunti/Feltrinelli. Besides novels she writes screenplays, coffee table books, travel books and tourist guides, focusing her attention on the great cities of the world, cinema and music, animals and nature. In 2014 she won the "First Place for 2013" in "Personality Profile - International Journalism" at the 56th Annual Southern California Journalism Awards in Los Angeles and she finished the screenplay based on her novel *Storie di New York* (Stories of New York, 2010), together with the American screenplaywriter Lucy Ridolphi. For White Star Publishers she published *Wonders of New York* and *Australia, the New Frontier*.

The Author would like to thank the following persons for their assistance in editing:
Lucy Ridolphi (the entire book); Paula Llavallol (first draft of certain chapters);
Valerie Geiss (first draft of the Robert De Niro and Woody Allen chapters).

Photographic Credits

AA World Travel Library/Alamy/IPA: page 189
Ajansen/iStockphoto: page 132
Alessandra Mattanza: pages 7, 31, 82-83, 107, 115, 117, 122, 123, 124, 125, 133, 136-137, 155, 169, 179, 232, 234
Alfredo Maiquez/Agefotostock: page 235
Allgöver Walter/Marka: page 158
Alvaro Leiva/Agefotostock: page 248
Alvaro Leiva/Marka: page 237
Andrew Burton/Getty Images: pages 40-41
Andrew Cribb/iStockphoto: page 252
Andrew H. Walker/Getty Images: page 81
Andrew Kazmierski/123RF: pages 130-131
Andria Patino/Agefotostock: page 109
Anna Bryukhanova/iStockphoto: page 209
Atlantide Phototravel/Corbis: pages 12-13, 138

Bartomeu Amengual/Agefotostock: pages 146-147
Bettmann/Corbis: page 233
Bilderbox/Agefotostock: page 249
Blickwinkel/Agefotostock: page 77
Bo Zaunders/Corbis: page 47
Brad Rickerby/Marka: pages 4-5
Brian Jannsen/Alamy/IPA: page 217
Brian Lawrence/Getty Images: pages 140-141
Bruno Barbey/Magnum Photo/Contrasto: page 143
Bryan Busovicki/123RF: page 152
Camera Press/Nick Wilson/Contrasto: page 87
Cameron Davidson/Corbis: page 16
Carson1984/123RF: page 24
Cem Ozdel/Anadolu Agency/Getty Images: page 182
Chee-Onn Leong/123RF: page 197
Christophe d'Yvoire/Sygma/Corbis: page 15

Christopher Anderson/Magnum/Contrasto: page 207
Cindy Ord/Getty Images: page 85
Citizen of the Planet/Alamy/IPA: page 22
Timothy A. Clary/AFP/Getty Images: pages 26-27
Craftvision/iStockphoto: page 32
CribbVisual/iStockphoto: pages 118-119
Daniel Schoenen/imageBROKER/Agefotostock: pages 25, 253
Danita Delimont/Getty Images: page 225
David Grossman/Alamy/IPA: pages 50, 110, 111, 190
David LEFRANC/Gamma-Rapho via Getty Images: pages 18-19
Dell640/iStockphoto: page 163
Doug Pearson/Getty Images: pages 70, 241
Ellisphotos/Alamy/IPA: page 186

All the texts and interviews have been approved
by the people Alessandra Mattanza interviewed.
To be as accurate as possible all the interviewees
have been asked to read and approve every text-interview
for publication. We apologize for any inaccurate
information and welcome corrections,
which will be made in future editions.

WHITE STAR PUBLISHERS

WS White Star Publishers® is a registered trademark
property of De Agostini Libri S.p.A.

© 2015 De Agostini Libri S.p.A.
Via G. da Verrazano, 15
28100 Novara, Italy
www.whitestar.it - www.deagostini.it

ISBN 978-88-544-0855-5
1 2 3 4 5 6   19 18 17 16 15

Printed in China